The Coronation of King Charles III

A New Era for the United Kingdom

As you start reading this book, you'll embark on a journey through the fascinating history and culture of the United Kingdom. With each page, you'll discover fresh insights and perspectives, revealing the customs and traditions that have influenced this country throughout its history. By the time you reach the end of the book, you'll have a deeper understanding and appreciation of the United Kingdom and its significance in today's world.

By: Fulton J. Titus

Atlas Press Publishing, LLC

9206 Avenue K

Brooklyn, NY 11236

For information about special discounts for bulk purchases, please contact Atlas Press Publishing LLC: Www.AtlasPressLLC.com Email: Info@AtlasPressLLC.com or AtlasPressAd@gmail.com

To my dear children Sephora, Logan, and Savannah,

As I bring this book into the world, I dedicate it to the three of you with all my heart. Your unwavering love, support, and encouragement have been the fuel that has driven me to see this project to fruition. Through your eyes, I have been able to see the world in a new light, and it is your presence that has given me the strength to persevere in times of doubt.

As you hold this book in your hands, know that it is a testament to the love that we share as a family. My hope is that through the pages of this book, you will be able to glimpse a world that is full of wonder and magic, and that it will inspire you to chase after your dreams with the same fervor that I have chased after mine.

I am eternally grateful to have you as my children, and I look forward to seeing the beautiful futures that await each and every one of you.

With all my love,

The Coronation of King Charles III
A New Era for the United Kingdom

Experience the magic of an Atlas Press Publishing Production

AtlasPress
- PUBLISHING. LLC -

By: Fulton J. Titus

Acknowledgements

I would like to express my gratitude to all those who have supported me in the writing of this book. Firstly, I would like to thank my family and friends for their unwavering support and encouragement throughout the writing process. Without their support, this book would not have been possible.

I would also like to extend my thanks to the many experts in the fields of history, culture, and the arts who have shared their knowledge and insights with me, enriching the content of this book.

Finally, I would like to thank the readers for their interest in this book. It is my sincere hope that you find it informative and engaging, and that it inspires you to explore the fascinating history and culture of the United Kingdom.

Fulton J. Titus

Words cannot express how thankful I am to Atlas Press Publishing for their resolute support and dedication to bringing this book to life. Without their expertise, guidance, and commitment to excellence, this project would not have been possible. Their professionalism and attention to detail have been instrumental in making this book a reality, and I am honored to have had the opportunity to work with such a fantastic team. Thank you, Atlas Press Publishing, for all that you have done to make this book a success.

Fulton J. Titus

Table of Contents

The Coronation of King Charles III

A New Era for the United Kingdom

By: Fulton J. Titus

Preface

Behold! The coronation of a new monarch - a momentous occasion that captures the world's attention and ignites a flame in the hearts of passionate royal family enthusiasts. It's a celebration of tradition, history, and the promise of a new era, infused with the buzz and frenzied energy of social media, the internet, text messages, and the 24-hour news cycle.

As the United Kingdom prepares for the coronation of King

Charles III, the world eagerly awaits this historic event, poised to embark on a journey of discovery and excitement. In this book, we invite you to join us on a deep dive into the life of King Charles III, exploring his accomplishments, relationships, philanthropic and environmental pursuits, sense of humor, wealth, race relations, and much more.

We meticulously examine the historical context and significance of the coronation ceremony, from the intricate preparations and logistics to the rituals and customs that are an intrinsic part of the event. We also dive into the perspectives of the British people and the press regarding this grand occasion, exploring the fervor and passion that grips the nation in anticipation of the coronation.

This is not just a ceremonial event; the coronation has significant political and international implications. We take an in-depth look into the potential economic impact of the coronation, as well as the impact on the royal family and the perspective of the business community.

As we look forward to the coronation of King Charles III, we recognize the importance of this event in shaping the future of the United Kingdom and the world. This book serves as a valuable resource for anyone interested in the rich history of the United Kingdom, the monarchy, and the perspectives of the British people and the press. Join us on this thrilling journey of discovery and passion, as we explore the life and legacy of King Charles III and the momentousness of the coronation ceremony. Do not miss the opportunity to be a part of this history-making event.

King Charles

Introduction

The Coronation of King Charles III: "A New Era for the United Kingdom". It's an enthralling exploration of the most remarkable event in the history of the United Kingdom. Delving deep into the heart of this grand ceremonial event, marinated in history, it marks the dawning of a new chapter in the country's story. This book takes a captivating look at the coronation's rich history in the United Kingdom, ranging from the first recorded coronation of King Edgar in 973 to the latest coronation of Queen Elizabeth II in 1953, and the upcoming coronation of King Charles III. It captures every detail, from the preparations and logistics of the event to the ceremony itself and its aftermath. Additionally, it provides an intriguing glimpse into King Charles III's background, views and future role as the monarch of the United Kingdom.

The book starts by offering an awe-inspiring overview of the monarchy and the vital role it has played in shaping the United Kingdom's history, from the Norman conquest[1] to the present day. The reader gains a fascinating understanding of how the monarchy evolved over time and its present-day role in the United Kingdom. It includes a historical account of previous coronations and their significance in the context of British history, painting a vivid picture of the splendor and importance of these grand ceremonial events.

The book then moves on to explore the planning and logistics of the coronation, providing a behind-the-scenes look at the role of government and other organizations in the preparations. The reader gains an exclusive inside look at the planning process, including the challenges that come with organizing such a grand event, and the economic impact of the event on the United Kingdom.

The reader also learns about the expected attendance, the security measures, and the expected media coverage of the event. It provides an insightful, detailed account of the preparations made to ensure that the event runs smoothly and the roles and responsibilities of the different organizations involved in the planning.

The centerpiece of the book is the detailed description of the coronation ceremony itself, taking place on May 06, 2023. The book provides a breathtaking, step-by-step account of the ceremony, from the day before the coronation, the monarch's arrival, to the anointing and the crowning function. It includes a fascinating overview of all the customs, traditions, and rituals that make the coronation such a grand and meaningful event. The reader is taken on an exciting journey through the symbols and meanings behind the rituals, with illustrations and photographs to help visualize the splendor of the celebration.

The book concludes with an examination of the coronation's impact on the United Kingdom and the world, including any political or social reforms that will occur as a result. It explores the celebrations and the public reaction to the event, as well as the impact on the economy and the tourism industry.

This book is a must-read for anyone captivated by the monarchy, British history, and the grandeur of coronations. It provides an in-depth guide to the event and a profound understanding of the history, practice, and substance of the coronation of King Charles III, and how it fits in the context of previous coronations in the UK. This is a book that will leave the reader feeling moved and inspired by the splendor and historical significance of the coronation ceremony.

The British Empire

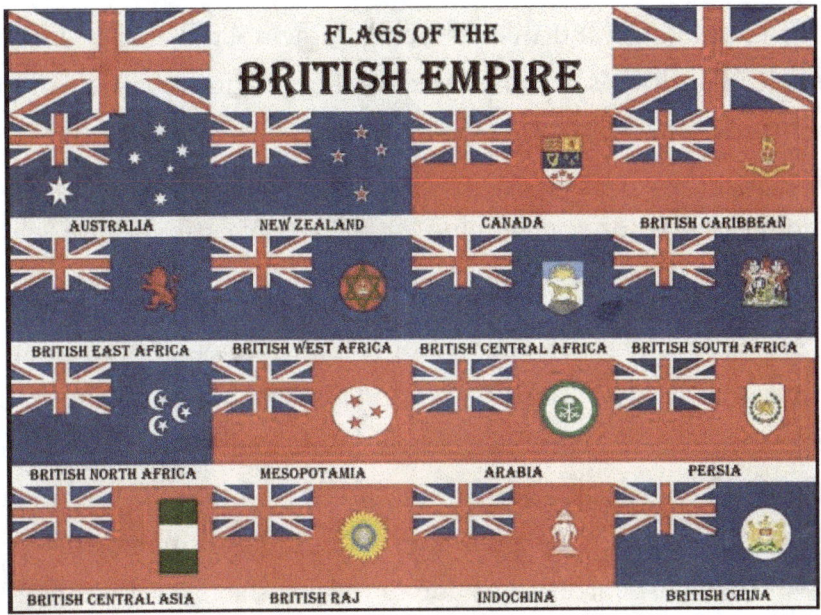

FLAGS OF THE
BRITISH EMPIRE

AUSTRALIA — NEW ZEALAND — CANADA — BRITISH CARIBBEAN

BRITISH EAST AFRICA — BRITISH WEST AFRICA — BRITISH CENTRAL AFRICA — BRITISH SOUTH AFRICA

BRITISH NORTH AFRICA — MESOPOTAMIA — ARABIA — PERSIA

BRITISH CENTRAL ASIA — BRITISH RAJ — INDOCHINA — BRITISH CHINA

B ritish history is a tapestry woven with the threads of monarchs and wars, conquests and evolution. The monarchy has played a central role in the history of the United Kingdom, from the Norman conquest to the present day. It's not a surprise that the coronation of a new king is a significant event in the history of the country and is unapologetically abundant in tradition and custom.

The practice of enthronement in the UK dates back to the

10th century when King Edgar was crowned in 973. Since then, there have been numerous coronations, each one with its own unique account and impact on the country. Some of the most memorable coronations in British history include that of King William the Conqueror in 1066, Queen Elizabeth II in 1953, and King George VI in 1937.

The love for the king is an enduring theme in British history, with many kings and queens being remembered fondly by the people. This love is not just based on the constitutional role of the monarchy, but also on the personal characteristics of the monarchs themselves. A king who is seen as a strong leader, a good communicator, or a champion of the people can inspire great loyalty and affection among the population.

The crowning of a king is not just a ceremonial event, but it also marks a new chapter in the history of the country. It represents a new beginning, a new hope, and a new era for the nation. The upcoming investiture of King Charles III will be no different. Some might argue that it would be of greater historic fervor than past coronations due to the press and our love for 24-hour news cycles.

The inauguration of King Charles III is an historic event that will attract the attention of the world. With the royal family's popularity reaching new heights in recent years, millions of people are expected to tune in to watch the ceremony. The coronation will take place at Westminster Abbey, the same location where every British monarch has been crowned since 1066.

Westminster Abbey is one of the most iconic landmarks in London and is macerated in history. The abbey has been the site of many historic events over the centuries, including the coronation and the funeral of Queen Elizabeth II, the funeral of Princess Diana, and the wedding of Prince William and Kate Middleton. The building itself is a marvel of Gothic architecture, with soaring ceilings and intricate stone carvings that leave visitors in awe.

The ceremony itself is submerged in tradition and is a sight to behold. The coronation begins with the royal procession, where the king is escorted to Westminster Abbey by the Household Cavalry. The procession is a spectacle of pomp and ceremony, with soldiers in full regalia and a sea of Union Jack flags waving in the wind.

Once inside the abbey, the king takes his place on the coronation chair, a throne made of oak that dates back to the 14th century. The Archbishop of Canterbury then performs the coronation ceremony, which includes the anointing of the king with holy oil and the crowning of the monarch with the St. Edward's Crown, a symbol of the monarch's authority.

The anointing of King Charles III is not just a celebration of the monarchy, but also a celebration of British culture and tradition. The coronation will be a time for the people of Britain to come together and celebrate their shared heritage and values. It will be a time for reflection on the past and a time to look towards the future with hope and optimism.

In recent years, the monarchy has enjoyed a resurgence in popularity, particularly among younger Britons. The royal family has worked hard to remain relevant in a rapidly changing world, and their efforts have paid off. From the Queen's Diamond Jubilee to the wedding of Prince Harry and Meghan Markle, the royal family has captured the hearts of the nation and the world. The younger generation of royals, including Prince William, Kate Middleton, Harry and Meghan, have brought a fresh and modern perspective to the monarchy, making it more relatable to a younger audience. Their popularity has also helped to boost the tourism industry in the UK, with visitors coming from all over the world to see Buckingham Palace, the Tower of London, and other royal landmarks.

Despite its popularity, the monarchy is not without its controversies. Prince Andrew's association with Jeffrey Epstein and the subsequent scandal has tarnished the royal family's reputation, leading some to question the institution's relevance in modern society. Additionally, there have been calls for the royal family to become more diverse and representative of the country's multicultural population. The appointment of Prince William as the first royal to speak out against racism and discrimination is a step in the right direction, but more work needs to be done.

Looking to the future, the upcoming public crowning of King Charles III will undoubtedly be a once-in-a-lifetime event in the history of the United Kingdom. The preparations for the coronation are already underway, and it is set to be a grand and elaborate affair, infused with tradition and history. From the ceremonial procession to the anointing with holy oil, every aspect of the coronation has a rooted emblematic meaning, reflecting the country's long and complex history.

As with any major event, there are concerns about security and safety. In the wake of recent terror attacks in the UK, authorities are taking extra precautions to ensure the coronation goes smoothly and safely. The event is expected to draw large crowds, both in London and around the world, and there will be heightened security measures in place to protect the public and the royal family.

But the inauguration is not just a day of opulence and circumstance. It is a time for reflection and renewal, a time for the country to come together and celebrate its history, traditions, and values. It is an opportunity for the monarchy to reaffirm its commitment to the people of the UK and to the world, and to set a positive tone for the future.

In addition to its ceremonial duties, the monarchy also has a constitutional role to play. The new King will act as a figurehead for the country and represents the United Kingdom on the world stage. King Charles will also serve as a figurehead of national unity and stability, which is particularly important during times of political uncertainty.

The upcoming crowning of King Charles III is expected to draw a large and enthusiastic crowd, with people from all over the country eager to take part in the celebrations. The event will be a chance for the people to come together and celebrate the history and traditions of the monarchy, as well as the unity of the country. It will also provide an opportunity to reflect on the importance of the coronation ceremony and its role in the history of the country.

The enthronement of a king or queen is a complex and highly ritualized event, with many different traditions and customs involved. From the crowning formality to the presentation of the royal regalia, every aspect of the coronation has its own symbolic meaning and weight. For example, the orb, scepter, and crown are all symbols of the monarch's power and authority, while the anointing with holy oil represents the monarch's divine right to rule.

While the festivities of the crowning of a new ruler are entrenched in tradition, there have been some changes to the event over the years. For example, the anointing oil used during the ceremony was changed in 1953 to ensure that it would not stain the monarch's clothing. The music played during the ritual has also been updated to reflect changing tastes and preferences.

In recent years, the monarchy has also faced some challenges and controversies. The younger members of the royal family have come under increased scrutiny from the media, and there have been calls for the monarchy to be abolished altogether. However, despite these challenges, the monarchy remains a beloved and enduring institution in British society.

Overall, the enthroning of King Charles III promises to be a historic and unforgettable event in the history of the United

Kingdom. It will be a chance for the people to come together and celebrate the traditions and customs of the monarchy, as well as the unity and strength of the country. While the monarchy has faced its fair share of challenges over the years, it continues to be an important and beloved part of British society, and the upcoming coronation will be a testament to that enduring legacy.

United Kingdom and Coronations

In the annals of British history, few events hold as much significance as the coronation. This grand occasion, immersed in tradition and symbolism, has been a fixture of British society since the early Middle Ages, serving as a powerful symbol of national unity, identity, and continuity. From the momentous coronation of William the Conqueror in 1066 to the dazzling spectacle of Queen Elizabeth II's crowning in 1953, coronations have remained a cornerstone of British culture, evoking a sense of glory and majesty that has captivated generations.

But what is it about coronations that inspire such awe and reverence? Is it the opulence of the ceremony, the splendor of the regalia, or the sheer magnitude of the event itself? Perhaps it is all of these things, and more. For in the coronation, we find not just a celebration of a new monarch, but a celebration of the very essence of the British nation – its history, its customs, its values, and its people.

Indeed, the role of the monarchy in promoting national unity in the United Kingdom cannot be overstated. The monarchy serves as a unifying force that brings together people from all corners of the country, transcending social, cultural, and political divides to forge a shared identity based on a deep reverence for tradition, heritage, and national pride. This is especially important in a rapidly changing world, where the need for stability and continuity is more acute than ever.

It is no wonder that the investiture has evolved over the centuries to reflect the changing political and cultural landscape of the United Kingdom. From the religious ceremonies and oaths of office of the Middle Ages to the pageantry and dazzle of the modern era, the coronation has remained a symbol of British identity and continuity, adapting to the needs of the times while staying true to its core purpose.

Now, as the reign of Queen Elizabeth II draws to a close, a new monarch stands poised to ascend the throne – King Charles III. The character of this future king, his strengths and weaknesses, his virtues and flaws, are the subject of much speculation and debate. But one thing is certain – his coronation will be an important rite, a symbol of continuity and renewal that will reaffirm the essential role of the monarchy in British society.

For the royal family, the anointing of King Charles III will be more than just a ceremonial event – it will be a reflection of their ongoing commitment to the people of the United Kingdom, a testament to the enduring bond that exists between the monarchy and the nation it serves. And for the people of the United Kingdom, the coronation will be a source of pride and inspiration, a chance to come together and celebrate their shared history and culture, and to look forward to a future filled with hope and promise.

But the substance of the coronation extends far beyond the borders of the United Kingdom. For tourists and visitors from around the world, the crowing of King Charles III will be a once-in-a-lifetime opportunity to witness a truly historic event, to glimpse the pageantry and splendor of British culture at its finest. It will be a chance to experience the magic and majesty of the British monarchy firsthand, marvel at the intricacy and symbolism of the coronation ceremony, and feel a sense of connection to the rich history and heritage of the United Kingdom.

In conclusion, the not to be missed, crowning of King Charles III will be a triumph of tradition, a celebration of continuity, and a symbol of national unity and pride. It will be a reminder that, no matter how much the world may change, the essence of the British nation remains constant – a deep reverence for history, culture, and tradition, and a commitment to the enduring values that have sustained the United Kingdom.

Importance Of UK To The World

The monarchy in the United Kingdom has a complex and multifaceted significance that is greatly ingrained in British culture, history, tradition, and customs. It is a symbol of continuity and stability, and a source of pride and affection for the British people. The monarchy is not just a political institution but a cultural and social one as well, closely associated with other institutions such as the Church of England, the Armed Forces, and the Commonwealth. The monarchy is also an important source of soft power for the United Kingdom, enhancing its global standing and influence. However, the monarchy's role is not just confined to domestic affairs. It also has a consequential impact on the international platform, representing the United Kingdom in diplomatic and political circles. The King or Queen is frequently observed as a symbol of steadiness and constancy, making the monarchy a salient figure in the eyes of other countries.

From the magnificence of the coronation to the spectacle of the annual Trooping the Colour, the monarchy is an integral part of British life and society. The Trooping of the Colour has "marked the official birthday of the British Sovereign" for over 260 years. Over 1400 parading soldiers, 200 horses and 400 musicians come together each June in a great display of military precision, horsemanship and fanfare to mark the Sovereign's official birthday. The upcoming date for this event is Sat, Jun 17, 2023 2:00 PM. Its role is not just ceremonial but also symbolic, representing the country as a whole and embodying the values and aspirations of the British people. As will be repeated over and over again throughout this book, the monarchy is enriched in history and tradition, and its customs and protocols are deeply respected and valued by the British people.

The monarchy has played a central role in the development of the British political system, providing a source of stability and continuity throughout the country's history. As a constitutional monarch, the King or Queen acts as a symbol of cultural solidarity, representing the nation's values and traditions. The monarchy is also an essential part of the country's identity and legacy, preserving its customs and culture for future generations.

The monarchy's unique position in the British constitutional system is the result of centuries of historical and legal developments, and its role has evolved over time. Today, the monarch and the royal family are British citizens, but they also occupy a special constitutional role with certain privileges and exemptions. While the royal family does not possess the same rights and freedoms as the general British population, they are also not subject to certain laws and taxes. For example, the monarch and their immediate family are exempt from paying income tax and the Grown Estate is exempt from inheritance tax. As the head of state, the monarch is considered the "fount of justice[1]" and is above the law in some respects, but is also subject to specific obligations and limitations as set out in the Constitution.

Despite its special status, the monarchy is not above criticism or controversy. There have been calls for the monarchy to be abolished or reformed, particularly in light of recent scandals

---

[1] In the United Kingdom, the concept of the "fount of justice" embodies the idea that the monarch is the ultimate source of justice and authority in the country. It symbolizes the monarch's constitutional role as the embodiment of the nation's history and traditions, and emphasizes the importance of the rule of law and the administration of justice. However, in practice, the administration of justice is carried out by the courts, which are independent of the monarchy and the government.

Thus, the "fount of justice" serves as a powerful reminder of the historical and symbolic importance of the monarchy in upholding the principles of justice and fairness. While the practical administration of justice is carried out by an independent judiciary, the symbolic role of the monarch in embodying these principles remains a crucial part of the country's legal and constitutional system. Overall, the concept of the "fount of justice" underscores the deep and enduring significance of the monarchy in British culture and history.

involving members of the royal family. However, such calls are often met with resistance from those who view the monarchy as an essential part of British identity and heritage.

The monarchy's origins can be discovered back to the time of the Roman conquest when Britain was first introduced to the concept of kingship. Over the centuries, the role of the monarchy has evolved, but it has remained a constant throughout the country's history, providing balance and dependability. The monarchy has also played a central role in the development of the country's political system, and today the King or Queen acts as a symbol of cultural solidarity.

As such members of the royal family including the monarch are not allowed to vote in elections. They are also not allowed to hold any political office or publicly express their political views. This is in line with the principle of the separation of powers, which states that the monarch should not interfere in the workings of the government. The monarchy's constitutional role as a neutral and non-partisan figurehead is also seen as an important safeguard against the excesses of party politics and the potential instability that can arise from political polarization. The monarchy is a salient symbol of territorial integrity and continuity, and it is believed that allowing members of the royal family to vote or hold political office would compromise this role.

In addition to its political and cultural importance, the monarchy is also an economic force in its own right. The Crown Estate, which is managed by an independent body, generates a good amount of revenue for the government and is responsible for the management of valuable properties and assets such as Buckingham Palace and Windsor Castle. The monarchy also attracts millions of tourists each year, generating revenue for the tourism industry and creating jobs and economic opportunities in the process.

The monarchy's impact on British society and culture cannot be overstated. It is a symbol of national pride and cultural solidarity, representing the country's values and aspirations. Its role in preserving British customs and culture is evident in the numerous palaces and castles that are open to the public, which serves as a reminder of the country's rich history and heritage.

The monarchy's cultural meaning can also be observed in the country's traditions and ceremonies. The Changing of the Guard ceremony, for example, is a long-standing tradition that takes place daily at Buckingham Palace and is a popular tourist attraction. The commemoration involves the official handover of responsibility for the protection of the palace, and it is a display of the military and pageantry traditions that have been an integral part of British history for centuries.

The monarchy's historical role is also reflected in the country's architecture and art. Many of the country's iconic buildings, such as St Paul's Cathedral, Westminster Abbey, and the Tower of London, were built during the monarchy's reign and are a testament to the country's cultural and architectural heritage. Similarly, the monarchy has been a patron of the arts for centuries, and many of the country's most prominent cultural institutions, such as the Royal Opera House and the National Gallery, receive funding and support from the royal family.

The monarchy's role in British society extends beyond its cultural and historical noteworthiness. The monarchy also has a great deal of economic impact on the country, both through its tourism industry and its contribution to the country's trade and commerce. According to a report by Brand Finance, the monarchy's brand value was estimated to be £67.5 billion in 2020, with the tourism industry alone contributing an estimated £2.7 billion to the country's economy.

The monarchy's economic significance is not limited to tourism, however. The royal family also plays an active role in promoting British businesses and trade, both domestically and internationally. The Queen, for example, hosted an annual reception for British business leaders, and the royal family frequently undertake trade missions abroad to promote British products and services.

The United Kingdom is a country that holds remarkable importance on the world platform, with its history, culture, and global influence. The country has a long and rich history of diplomacy, international relations, and trade, making it an influential player in global affairs. The UK has strong and diverse relationships with various countries around the world, including the United States, Europe, and the Commonwealth, among others.

One of the most crucial relationships that the UK holds is with the United States. The two countries have a "special relationship" which is rooted in their shared history, values and interest. The UK and the US have had a close relationship for over a century; the UK is the United States' closest ally and the two countries work closely together on a range of issues, including defense and security, trade and investment, and global challenges such as climate change and the COVID-19 pandemic. For example, in the aftermath of the 9/11 world trade center attacks in America, the UK and the US worked closely together to combat terrorism and the UK has been a key partner in the fight against ISIS. The two countries have been allies in times of war and peace, and they have worked together to promote democracy, human rights, and free trade. The special relationship between the UK and the US has been a cornerstone of their foreign policies and it has helped shape the world order in the post-World War II era.

Another critical relationship that the UK has is with the European Union (EU) which it joined in 1973. As a member of the EU, the UK was part of a single market and customs union, which facilitated trade and investment across the continent. The EU also provided the UK with a platform to work with other European countries on issues such as climate change, migration, and security. The UK's relationship with the EU has been complex, but it has been an essential part of the country's foreign policy for decades. The UK was a member of the EU for over 40 years, during which it helped shape the bloc's policies and institutions. However, in 2016, the UK held a referendum on its membership in the EU, and the majority of the British people voted to leave the bloc. Since then, the UK has been negotiating its exit from the EU, which has been a complex and challenging process.

Despite leaving the EU, the UK maintains close ties with Europe, including its military alliance, NATO. The UK and the other NATO member states work together to promote global security and stability. The UK has also been a crucial player in the fight against terrorism and international crime, working closely with its European partners to combat these threats.

The UK also has a long and historic relationship with the Commonwealth[2], a group of 54 countries that were formerly part of the British Empire. The Commonwealth provides a platform

---

[2] The Commonwealth of Nations, often referred to simply as the Commonwealth, is an association of 54 independent states that are mostly former territories of the British Empire. The United Kingdom is one of the founding members of the Commonwealth, and has played a central role in its development and evolution over the years.

The Commonwealth is united by shared values and principles, including democracy, human rights, and the rule of law. It provides a forum for countries to work together on issues of mutual interest, such as trade, education, and cultural exchange. The Queen is the ceremonial head of the Commonwealth, and plays an important role in promoting its values and goals.

While the Commonwealth is not a political or military alliance, it has played a significant role in shaping the international landscape, particularly in the post-colonial era. It has been a force for promoting democracy and human rights, and has helped to foster cooperation and understanding among its member states. The relationship between the United Kingdom and the Commonwealth reflects the country's historical ties to its former colonies, and underscores the importance of shared values and cultural heritage in shaping the global community.

for its members to work together on issues such as trade, education, and development. The UK also plays a major role in the United Nations (UN), where it is a permanent member of the Security Council. As a member of the Security Council, the UK has played a key role in promoting peace and security around the world, including in Syria, Yemen, and the Korean Peninsula.

The Commonwealth is a voluntary association of independent countries that share a common language, history, and culture. The UK has been a vital member of the Commonwealth since its inception, and it has played a memorable role in shaping the organization's policies and initiatives. The Commonwealth has been a platform for the UK to promote democracy, human rights, and economic development in member countries.

In addition to these relationships, the UK also has important ties with other countries around the world, including China, India, and Japan. These countries are noteworthy players in the global economy, and the UK works closely with them to promote trade and investment. The UK has also been a leader in promoting environmental sustainability and combating climate change, working closely with other countries to find solutions to these pressing issues.

It should be expressed that the UK has important ties to Africa. The UK and Africa have a long history of collaboration, and the UK is committed to strengthening its relationship with African nations.

One example of the UK's important ties to Africa is its

investment in the continent. The UK is one of the largest investors in Africa, with important investments in sectors such as energy, infrastructure, and healthcare. For example, in 2021, the UK announced a £200 million investment in Africa's renewable energy sector, which will help to address the continent's energy deficit and support economic growth.

Another example of the UK's important ties to Africa is its development assistance. The UK is a major donor of aid to Africa, providing impressive support for health, education, and economic development initiatives. For instance, the UK has pledged £1.4 billion in aid to help girls in developing countries access education, including in Africa. The UK also provides support for initiatives aimed at tackling poverty and improving economic development in African countries.

Finally, the UK is an important partner for African countries in the area of security. The UK has played a key role in supporting peacekeeping efforts in Africa and has provided training and support for African military and security forces. For example, the UK is currently supporting the African Union Mission in Somalia (AMISOM), which is working to stabilize the country and support its government.

Overall, the UK's relationships with other countries are diverse and critical to the country's foreign policy and global influence. These relationships are based on shared values, interests, and history, and they help promote peace, stability, and prosperity around the world. The UK is a major player in global affairs, and its partnerships with other countries are vital to its continued success and relevance at the international spotlight.

The Rich History of
The United Kingdom

The United Kingdom's rich and diverse history spans thousands of years, and the role of the monarchy has been central throughout this history. From the earliest known human presence in the region in around 8000 BC to the present day, the UK's history is a tapestry of different civilizations, invasions, and cultures that have shaped the country and its people. The monarchy has played an influential role in this, and its history is peppered with important examples of creative and memorable events.

One of the earliest recorded periods in the UK's history is that of the Celtic tribes[3] who settled in the region around 600 BC. The Celtic way of life had a considerable influence on the region, and many of its customs and traditions still exist today. Some of the famous things that the Celtic tribes created include intricate metalwork, such as jewelry and weapons, as well as distinctive art styles that featured abstract patterns and symbols. The Celts also had a rich oral tradition, and their stories and myths have survived through the ages. During this period, the monarchy served as a representative of stability and consistency.

Following the Celtic period, the Roman Empire[4] conquered

---

[3] The Celtic tribes were early inhabitants of the British Isles, and their presence can be traced back to at least the 6th century BC. The tribes were organized into various kingdoms and were known for their distinct cultures and linguistic practices, which included the use of iron tools and weapons, farming, and storytelling.
The Celtic tribes were eventually conquered by the Romans in the 1st century AD, and their influence gradually diminished over time. However, their cultural legacy can still be seen today in the languages, customs, and traditions of the people of the United Kingdom, particularly in Scotland, Wales, and Cornwall, where Celtic heritage is particularly strong.

[4] The Roman Empire was a vast and powerful state that existed from 27 BCE to 476 CE, and encompassed much of Europe, the Middle East, and North Africa. It was founded by the first emperor, Augustus, and lasted for over five centuries. The empire was known for its sophisticated legal system, impressive architecture, and military might, and was a major influence on Western values and civilization.

and occupied the region for nearly four centuries, leaving behind a legacy of engineering, architecture, and language. Although the Roman Empire did not have a monarchy as we know it today, the role of the head of state was held by the Emperor. One of the most iconic events during this period was the construction of Hadrian's Wall, which served as a defensive fortification against invading tribes from the north.

The Anglo-Saxon period, which began in the 5th century AD, saw the arrival of Germanic tribes who established their own kingdoms and brought their own lifestyles and legacy. One of the most notable contributions of the Anglo-Saxons was their language, Old English, which laid the foundation for the development of the English language. They also left their mark on literature with famous works such as Beowulf, one of the oldest surviving epic poems in English literature. The Anglo-Saxon period was also marked by the arrival of Christianity, which would become the dominant religion in the region for centuries to come. During this period, the monarchy served as a symbol of national heritage and conformity.

The Norman Conquest in 1066 brought about extraordinary changes in the country, as the Normans brought with them a new language, movement, and political system. The Normans also built many castles and fortifications, which can still be seen today, such as the Tower of London. The Battle of Hastings was one of the most exceptional events of this period, as it marked the end of Anglo-Saxon rule and the beginning of Norman dominance.

Throughout the Middle Ages, the monarchy played a central role in the political and social landscape of the country, as kings and queens ruled and made decisions that impacted the country and its people. The monarchy also played a paramount role in the development of the country's political system, and the Magna Carta, signed in 1215 by King John, was a pivotal moment in the establishment of individual rights and freedoms.

In the modern day, the monarchy still holds an impressive role in the United Kingdom. The last official monarchy, under Queen Elizabeth II, has been a symbol of continuity and stability, and her reign has been marked by significant events such as the Golden Jubilee, the Diamond Jubilee, and the marriage of Prince William and Kate Middleton. Now, after the passing of Queen Elizabeth, Charles III will take the reign.

In conclusion, the monarchy continues to play a robust role in the modern day as a symbol of cohesion and uniformity, and it continues to play a function in the preservation of the country's heritage and customs. As the United Kingdom prepares to welcome a new king, it is a time of reflection on the past, present, and future of this great nation and the monarchy that has been an integral part of its history.

The New Monarchy
and The Economy

The monarchy is a vital component of the British economy, particularly in the tourism industry. Tourists from all over the world are drawn to the royal family's popularity and the phenomenon of coronations, eager to learn more about British history and the historical context of coronations. This generates a good amount of revenue for the country and provides a boost to the wealth and resources of the country as a whole.

An enthronement is a crucial event that can have a positive impact on the British economy, particularly through tourism. The UK has a rich history and heritage, which makes it an attractive destination for tourists from around the world. As such, a coronation can attract large numbers of visitors to the country, improving the overall Gross Domestic Product (G.D.P.) of the country by increasing demand for accommodation, transportation, and other tourism-related services.

In the lead-up to the inauguration, there will be a lot of media coverage and interest in the event. This generates curiosity and interest, increasing the number of visitors coming to the UK to witness the coronation. The event is an excellent opportunity to showcase the country's rich history and heritage, which can encourage more visitors to explore the UK's cultural attractions and landmarks in the near or long term.

Furthermore, a coronation can be an opportunity for the UK to showcase its value and history to the world through exhibitions, events, and other activities that can be organized around the event. This can help amplify the country's reputation as a tourist destination and attract more visitors in the future.

The impact of the anointing is not only felt in the tourism sector but also in other sectors of the economy. For instance, the retail sector is boosted as people buy souvenirs and memorabilia-related items to commemorate the event. Additionally, it provides a stimulus to the catering and hospitality sectors as people attend events and parties related to the coronation.

Historically, foreign visitors to the UK have been primarily from Europe, but there has been a heightened increase in the number of visitors from Asia and the Middle East in recent years. The UK's royal family is an attraction to people from all over the world. The crowning act of a new monarch is a glaring event that can attract visitors from all continents, including North and South America, Africa, Asia, and Australia.

Visitors from different countries may have unique reasons for visiting the UK. For example, some visitors may be attracted to the country's history and heritage, while others may be interested in attending the coronation ceremony itself. Some may also come to see the Crown Jewels, which are on display in the Tower of London. Regardless of the reason, the handover of power to a new monarch is likely to attract a diverse range of visitors from around the world.

The economic impact of a coronation on the UK is significant. According to a report by the Office for National Statistics (ONS), tourism accounts for nearly 10% of the country's GDP, and it is a crucial sector for job creation. Therefore, a coronation can create employment opportunities in various sectors of the economy, including accommodation, food and beverage, transportation, retail, and others.

In addition to the economic benefits, a coronation is a cultural event that brings the country together. It is an opportunity for people to come together to celebrate the coronation of a new monarch, witness history, and enjoy the festivities. It provides a sense of unity and pride in the country's heritage and traditions, which is essential for national identity and social cohesion.

The consequence of the crowning of a new monarch goes beyond just the economic benefits. It is a cultural phenomenon that has been celebrated in the UK for centuries. It is an event that connects the country's past, present, and future.

Furthermore, the coronation can also have a positive impact on the country's soft power. Soft power refers to the ability of a country to influence others through attraction and persuasion rather than through military or economic means. A successful coronation can enhance the country's reputation and prestige, and make it more attractive to foreign investors, diplomats, and policymakers. This can ultimately lead to more opportunities for economic and political cooperation with other countries.

When it comes to foreign visitors, the UK has a long history of attracting tourists from all over the world. In 2019, the top three countries for international visitors to the UK were the United States, France, and Germany. These countries have a strong interest in the UK's history, culture, and heritage, and a coronation can be a monumental draw for these visitors.

The US has a particularly strong fascination with the British monarchy, due in part to the country's shared history with the UK. American visitors have been known to travel to the UK specifically to witness major royal events, such as the wedding of Prince Harry and Meghan Markle in 2018. In fact, it has been estimated that the wedding generated around £1 billion in revenue for the UK economy.

French and German visitors are also likely to be drawn to the celebration of the crowning, as both countries have strong cultural and historical ties to the UK. French visitors may be interested in the Norman Conquest and the subsequent Norman influence on English culture, while German visitors may be drawn to the close historical and cultural ties between the two countries.

In addition to these countries, visitors from other parts of Europe, as well as from countries such as China, Australia, Canada and some African nations, are likely to be attracted to a coronation. These visitors may be interested in the glitter and ceremony of the event, as well as the historical and cultural significance of the British monarchy.

In terms of revenue, the economic impact of a coronation can be lucrative to the country. As mentioned earlier, the wedding of Prince Harry and Meghan Markle generated around £1 billion in revenue for the UK economy. A coronation, which is a much larger and more robust event, could generate even more revenue.

Moreover, a coronation can provide opportunities for businesses to showcase their products and services to a global audience. For example, luxury brands and high-end retailers can use the event to promote their products to high-net-worth individuals who are likely to attend the coronation.

In any event, an enthroning is not just a notable cultural event for the locals, but it also has the potential to provide a major economic boost to the UK. The event can attract visitors from around the world, promote the country's history and heritage, and provide opportunities for economic and political cooperation with other countries. As such, a coronation is a major opportunity for the UK to showcase its strengths and enhance its reputation at the global level.

The International Community and The Monarch

The monarchy, an institution rooted in tradition, is not just confined to the borders of the United Kingdom but extends its influence to other nations around the world. The Commonwealth countries, in particular, are imbued with historical connections to the British monarchy and continue to hold it in high regard as a symbol of continuity and stability. It is a testament to the importance and centrality of the monarchy in shaping the world and its place in the international community.

The immersion of a monarch in the international arena takes

many forms, from state visits to attendance at international events and conferences. By engaging in such activities, a monarch can assert their nation's interests and values and enhance their international profile. They can also build and strengthen diplomatic relationships with other countries, promoting cooperation and understanding.

Queen Elizabeth II, a monarch known for her longevity and commitment to duty, has traveled extensively during her reign, undertaking numerous state visits to countries such as the United States, Australia and Canada, among others. During these visits, she has met with foreign leaders and engaged in various cultural and diplomatic events, such as state banquets and the opening of new facilities and so on... This has helped to cement diplomatic relations between nations, promoting peace and stability on the global stage.

Other monarchs, such as King Felipe VI of Spain and King Willem-Alexander of the Netherlands, have similarly traveled abroad to participate in international events and forge new relationships with other nations. Their involvement in international diplomacy has helped to promote their countries' interests and values and build relationships of mutual respect and trust with other nations.

Beyond these formal diplomatic activities, monarchs can also use their international platform to support important social and humanitarian causes. Prince Harry, a member of the British royal family, has been a vocal advocate for mental health and has supported veterans and their families. Queen Rania of Jordan has been a fierce advocate for education and women's rights, using her position to promote positive change in her country and around the world.

Through their involvement in international diplomacy and support for social and humanitarian causes, monarchs can enhance their standing and influence on the world scale. They can demonstrate their commitment to promoting peace and prosperity and building bridges between nations, setting an example for all to follow. As such, the monarchy's influence extends far beyond its borders and continues to shape the world in profound ways. Additionally, the UK's role in World War II and the defeat of Nazi Germany under the leadership of Prime Minister Winston Churchill was another pivotal moment in the country's history.

In today's globalized world, the impact of a monarch's international presence and influence cannot be underestimated. The monarchy's ability to transcend national borders and connect with people from all over the world is a testament to its enduring relevance and importance.

Furthermore, the monarchy's reach extends beyond politics and diplomacy. It also has a crucial impact on popular culture and the arts. From literature to film and television, the monarchy has served as a rich source of inspiration and subject matter for artists and storytellers.

For instance, the recent hit Netflix series "The Crown" has

captivated audiences worldwide with its portrayal of the reign of Queen Elizabeth II and the inner workings of the royal family. Similarly, numerous books and films have been made about various members of the monarchy throughout history, further cementing their place in popular culture.

In addition to their cultural impact, the monarchy also plays an appreciable role in the British economy. The tourism industry, in particular, benefits greatly from the popularity of the royal family and associated events and attractions.

As previously indicated, visitors from around the world flock to the United Kingdom to catch a glimpse of the monarchy in action, whether it's at Buckingham Palace or one of the many events and ceremonies they participate in throughout the year. This generates a significant amount of revenue for the country and provides a boost to the wealth and resources of the country as a whole.

Overall, the monarchy's influence is felt in every aspect of British society, from politics and diplomacy to culture and economics. Its legacy and impact will continue to be felt for generations to come, both in the United Kingdom and around the world.

Who Is Prince Charles III

Prince Charles, the scion of the House of Windsor, is an enigmatic figure with a rich legacy that spans over seven decades. He is the eldest son of Queen Elizabeth II and Prince Philip, Duke of Edinburgh, and has been groomed since birth to be the future King of England. His parents' union, which has endured for over 70 years, has produced four children, including Charles, Princess Anne, Prince Andrew, and Prince Edward.

Since his birth on November 14, 1948, Charles has been destined for greatness, groomed for the role of King of England from the very beginning. He was raised in the spotlight, constantly under the scrutiny of the public eye, as he prepared to inherit the throne of the British monarchy. Throughout his life, he has been guided by the unwavering support and love of his parents, Queen Elizabeth II offering him guidance and support and Prince Philip, Duke of Edinburgh, who has instilled in him the values and virtues necessary to lead a nation.

But Charles is much more than a prince or an heir to the throne. He is a man of great accomplishments, a man of many passions, who has dedicated his life to the service of his country and his people. He received his education at Gordonstoun School, Scotland, and Trinity College, Cambridge, where he excelled academically and developed a keen interest in the arts and humanities.

Throughout his life, Charles has been involved in various initiatives and organizations, tirelessly working to make a difference in the world. He has served in the Royal Navy, dedicating himself to the service of his country, and has worked for numerous charities and organizations, championing causes close to his heart.

However, Charles' greatest legacy is his unwavering commitment to the environment and sustainable development. He is a staunch advocate for climate change and renewable energy, and has dedicated himself to promoting sustainable agriculture and the restoration and preservation of historic buildings. He has actively supported various arts organizations, using his position to champion the work of young and emerging artists, and has helped to highlight the importance of the arts in the UK and internationally.

As the new King of England, Charles is set to take on a whole new set of responsibilities and challenges. He will serve as the head of state, representing the country in international events, and will act as a symbol of national fellowship, bringing together the people of the United Kingdom in times of celebration and mourning. He will be involved in the work of various charities and organizations, both in the UK and internationally, and will use his position to promote causes that he is most passionate about, inspiring a new generation to take up the mantle of leadership and service.

In many ways, Charles' life has been one of service and devotion to others. He has dedicated himself to a range of charitable causes and organizations and has been a source of inspiration and hope for countless people around the world. His compassion, his empathy, and his unwavering commitment to making the world a better place have made him a beloved figure, and a symbol of hope and progress for all.

As Charles ascends to the throne, we can be confident that he will continue to serve with distinction and honor, and that he will work tirelessly to uphold the values and principles that have made the UK a beacon of hope and freedom throughout the world.

With his deep commitment to environmental sustainability, his unwavering dedication to the arts, and his steadfast compassion and empathy for all people, Charles is poised to lead the UK with grace, integrity, and honor.

Prince Charles III is set to become the oldest monarch in British history. This is an impressive feat that will cement his legacy as a crucial figure in the country's history. His age and experience have prepared him well for this role, and his years of service to the public make him a respected and beloved figure throughout the United Kingdom.

It is interesting to mention that the youngest monarch in British history was King Henry VI, who was just nine months old when he ascended the throne in 1422. Despite his young age, King Henry VI ruled for nearly 40 years, though his reign was marked by political instability and civil strife. In contrast, Prince Charles III has had a lifetime of preparation and is well-equipped to take on the responsibilities of the monarchy.

So let us hail the arrival of King Charles III, a man of great character, wisdom, and vision, who will lead his country with courage, compassion, and grace. Long may he reign, and long may his legacy endure!

The Educated Man

The importance of education is an essential part of life, and Charles, the Prince of Wales, has shown his dedication to this cause through his lifelong passion for learning. Throughout his academic career, he has amassed several degrees and diplomas that attest to his love of knowledge and his unrelenting pursuit of academic excellence.

From his early days at Hill House School and Cheam School

to his later years at Gordonstoun School, Charles has always been a devoted student. He then went on to attend Trinity College, Cambridge, where he earned a Bachelor of Arts degree in 1970. But Charles didn't stop there. His thirst for knowledge and passion for education pushed him further, and he pursued additional diplomas to bolster his academic credentials.

In 1971, Charles received a diploma in anthropology from Cambridge University, showcasing his interest in the study of humanity and culture. But he didn't stop there, as he also received a diploma in archaeology and anthropology from the same institution. Charles's passion for the study of the past and the ways in which it has influenced society has always been a driving force behind his academic pursuits.

Charles's dedication to education didn't end with his academic pursuits, as he has also been actively involved in several initiatives to advance learning. He has been a patron of several organizations that promote education, such as the Prince's Trust, which helps poor and untrained young people gain the skills and confidence they need to succeed in life. Charles's efforts to promote education show that he understands the power of knowledge and its transformative impact on individuals and society as a whole.

Interestingly, Charles is not the only member of the royal family with a passion for education. His niece, Princess Beatrice, also shares his passion and has been actively involved in promoting educational initiatives. In 2020, she became a patron of the Helen Arkell Dyslexia Charity, which provides support and resources for people with dyslexia. Like Charles, Princess Beatrice believes that education is the key to unlocking human potential and creating a better world for all.

Together, Charles and Princess Beatrice represent a powerful force for education, using their platform and influence to make education more accessible and help people achieve their full potential. Their dedication to education serves as an inspiration to all of us, reminding us of the transformative power of education and the importance of investing in the next generation.

In conclusion, Charles' unwavering commitment to education has been a constant source of inspiration and admiration. He has not only received several degrees and diplomas but has also actively worked to advance education and promote academic excellence. His dedication to education is a testament to his character and serves as a reminder of the importance of education in shaping and molding young minds.

The Queen and Charles

As the world's longest-reigning monarch, Queen Elizabeth II has presided over many changes in the royal family. Her eldest son, Prince Charles, has been at the forefront of these changes, and their relationship has been a subject of much discussion and speculation over the years.

Despite being a central figure in the royal family, Charles' relationship with his mother has been complex. While he has always been close to her, there have been reported tensions between the two over the years, especially regarding the role of the monarchy and the direction of the royal family. These tensions have been attributed to their different views on modernizing the monarchy and its institutions.

It is said that Charles has a more traditional view of the monarchy, which has led to disagreements with his mother over issues such as the role of the royal family in modern society, the handling of the royal finances, and the management of the royal estates. These differences have caused some observers to speculate about whether Charles will continue his mother's legacy or take the monarchy in a different direction.

However, despite these disagreements, Charles and the Queen have always maintained a close bond. They have been seen together at many public events, and the Queen has always been supportive of Charles and his role as the heir to the throne. Their relationship is one that is built on mutual respect and admiration, and it has stood the test of time.

Charles has also been a devoted son to the Queen throughout her reign. He has accompanied her on many engagements and events, and has always been supportive of her duty as the head of the royal family. His commitment to his mother and the monarchy is unwavering, and he has shown time and again that he is ready and willing to take on the responsibilities that come with being the future king.

In recent years, the royal family has undergone important changes, and Charles has been at the forefront of these changes. He has been actively involved in initiatives to modernize the monarchy and has been a strong advocate for causes such as environmentalism and sustainable living. His passion for these causes has made him a popular and respected figure, both within the royal family and in the wider public.

Despite their differences, the relationship between Charles

and the Queen was one that was built on a shared sense of duty and responsibility. Both have devoted their lives to serving their country and their people, and their commitment to this duty is unwavering. As the Queen entered the twilight of her reign, Charles took more of an active part in dealings of the monarchy. Based on what we know about the royal family, it is clear that the late Queen Elizabeth gave us a devoted and capable heir in her son Charles, who will continue to serve with distinction and honor.

In the lead-up to his ascension to the throne, King Charles III engaged in a period of mourning and reflection, paying tribute to his mother's life and service to the country that ended on September 8, 2022. Now he has taken the role of the king with the support of the royal family and the British people, and work to continue the legacy of the monarchy for generations to come.

Charles' Children

Charles, the Prince of Wales, has long been a prominent figure in the royal family. As the eldest child of Queen Elizabeth II, he has spent his entire life in the public eye and has been a central figure in British society. But while much is known about his public life, less is known about his private life and his relationship with his two sons, Prince William and Prince Harry.

Born on June 21, 1982, Prince William is the first child of Charles and Princess Diana. Charles was just 32 years old at the time, and had only recently married the beloved Princess. Despite his youth, Charles was already well-prepared for the responsibilities of fatherhood, and took an active role in William's upbringing and education from an early age.

As William grew older, Charles became more involved in his life, attending school events, sports matches, and other important milestones. He was determined to be a hands-on father and spent as much time with his son as possible. Charles also made sure that William received the best possible education, sending him to some of the country's most prestigious schools, including Eton College.

Despite his busy schedule and the demands of his royal duties, Charles remained committed to being a good father to William. He encouraged his son's interests and pursuits and took an active role in his development as a person. As William grew older and began to take on more responsibilities, Charles was there to guide him and offer his support.

But while Charles and William's relationship has always been close, his relationship with his younger son, Prince Harry, has been more complicated. Born on September 15, 1984, Harry was the second child of Charles and Princess Diana. But by the time he was born, Charles and Diana's marriage was already on the rocks, and their relationship was strained.

Despite this difficult start, Charles was determined to be a good father to Harry as well. He spent as much time with him as possible, attending school events and sports matches, and encouraging his interests and passions. Charles also made sure that Harry received a good education, sending him to the same prestigious schools as William.

However, the strain on Charles and Diana's relationship continued and eventually led to their separation and eventual divorce. For a time, Charles was a single father to William and Harry, a difficult and challenging role that he took on with grace and determination. Despite the challenges of being a single parent, Charles remained committed to his sons and did everything he could to provide them with love, support, and guidance.

In recent years, Charles's relationship with Harry has been tested once again, following Harry's decision to step back from his royal duties and move to North America with his wife, Meghan Markle. This decision, known as "Megxit"[5] was a difficult one for Charles, who had always hoped that his sons would follow in his footsteps and carry on the traditions of the royal family.

Despite these challenges, Charles has remained a devoted and

---

[5] The "Megxit" saga refers to the decision by Prince Harry and Meghan Markle, the Duke and Duchess of Sussex, to step back from their roles as senior members of the British royal family. In January 2020, the couple announced that they would be "financially independent" and divide their time between the United Kingdom and North America.

The decision came as a surprise to many, and was met with mixed reactions from the public and the media. The couple cited intense media scrutiny and a desire for privacy and independence as the reasons for their decision. Following negotiations with the royal family, it was announced that the couple would no longer use their HRH titles, and would no longer receive public funds. They also agreed to repay the cost of renovating their official residence, Frogmore Cottage. The couple has since launched various business ventures and charitable initiatives, and have made a new home for themselves in California.

loving father to both William and Harry. He continues to support them in their respective roles and pursuits and is always there for them when they need him. As he prepares to take on the responsibilities of the crown himself, Charles is determined to be the best father he can be to his two sons and to continue the legacy of the royal family for generations to come.

Lastly, the fact of the matter is to remember that the information available about Prince Charles' private life is limited to what is publicly known. While there are certainly many stories and rumors surrounding his personal life, it is impossible to know the full truth without being a part of his inner circle. As an outsider, all we can do is observe the public persona he presents and speculate on what might be going on behind closed doors. However, it is important to respect his privacy and not make assumptions or spread unfounded rumors. At the end of the day, Prince Charles is a human being with the right to his own personal life and we should respect that.

Charles, The Grandfather

As a grandfather, Prince Charles is known to embody the qualities of warmth, kindness, and patience, traits that he shares with, the Queen Mother. He is often seen interacting with his grandchildren with genuine interest and enthusiasm, imparting his wisdom and knowledge to them in a loving and gentle manner.

It is said that Prince Charles takes great pleasure in watching his grandchildren grow and learn, and he takes an active interest in their hobbies and passions. He is known to have a particular fondness for Prince George's love of soccer and Princess

Charlotte's love of dance, and he encourages them to pursue their interests with passion and dedication.

As a doting grandfather, Prince Charles is also known for his sense of humor and his ability to make his grandchildren laugh. He often tells them stories of his own childhood and shares his love of nature with them by taking them on walks in the countryside.

Furthermore, Prince Charles is deeply committed to preserving the environment for future generations, and he shares this passion with his grandchildren. He teaches them about the importance of sustainability and takes them on trips to see the natural wonders of the world.

It is also worth mentioning that Prince Charles has been a devoted single father to his own two sons, and this experience has undoubtedly influenced his role as a grandfather. He understands the importance of family and the value of spending time with loved ones, and he makes a concerted effort to be present in his grandchildren's lives.

In addition to his involvement in his grandchildren's lives, Prince Charles has also been a strong advocate for children's welfare and education. He is the patron of numerous charities and organizations that support children's well-being, and he has spoken publicly about the need to prioritize children's education and development.

Prince Charles' love for his grandchildren is evident in

everything he does, and his dedication to their well-being is unwavering. As he prepares to take the throne and assume his role as King, there is no doubt that he will continue to be a devoted grandfather, providing his grandchildren with love, support, and guidance as they navigate the challenges of life.

Charles, The Philanthropic

The exalted King Charles has a well-established record of being a philanthropist and has extended a helping hand to numerous charitable organizations throughout his life. His charitable endeavors have been wide-ranging, notable and beneficial for society. Some of his remarkable philanthropic endeavors are as follows:

1. The Prince's Trust: This remarkable charity was

established by Prince Charles in 1976 with a vision to assist young individuals who come from underprivileged backgrounds to develop their skills and to achieve their aspirations. The charity extends financial aid, training, and mentoring to the young ones and has successfully supported over one million young individuals to date.

2. The Prince's Charities: This is a group of not-for-profit organizations that were established by the Prince himself to address a diverse range of social, economic, and environmental issues. The charities are particularly focused on areas like education, health, and the arts, and work in collaboration with other organizations to achieve their objectives.

3. The Prince's Rainforest Project: An initiative launched by Prince Charles in 2007, this project endeavors to raise awareness about the importance of safeguarding rainforests and their critical role in mitigating climate change. The project collaborates with governments, businesses, and communities to promote sustainable development and protect the rainforests.

4. The Prince's Regeneration Trust: Established by Prince Charles in 1991, this charity aims to preserve and revitalize historic buildings and communities in the UK. The trust has successfully regenerated many historic buildings and communities, created employment opportunities for locals, and facilitated economic development.

5. The Prince's Foundation for Building Community: This charity was established by Prince Charles in 1986 to promote sustainable design and conventional architecture. The foundation works with architects, designers, and builders to develop sustainable building practices and promote the use of time-honored building techniques.

6. The Prince's Foundation for Children and the Arts: This is a charity founded by Prince Charles in 2002, which aims to introduce needy children to the arts. The foundation provides opportunities for children to attend concerts, theaters, museums, and other cultural events, which they may not have access to otherwise. The foundation believes that exposure to the arts can help to improve children's confidence, creativity, and overall well-being.

7. The British Asian Trust: Prince Charles is the founder of this organization, which was established in 2007 to support poverty-stricken communities in South Asia. The trust focuses on issues such as education, livelihoods, and mental health, and works with local partners to implement sustainable solutions.

8. The Prince's Farm Resilience Programme: This initiative was launched by Prince Charles in 2016 to support family farms in the UK. The program provides training and support to help farmers improve their business skills, increase their resilience, and adapt to changing market conditions.

9. The Prince of Wales's Corporate Leaders Group: This is a group of business leaders who work together to promote sustainable business practices and address climate change. The group was founded by Prince Charles in 2005 and has since become an influential voice in the business community.

10. The Prince of Wales's International Sustainability Unit: This is a group that was set up by Prince Charles in 2010 to promote sustainable development and address environmental issues at an international level. The unit works with governments, businesses, and civil society organizations to develop sustainable solutions to global challenges.

Apart from these noteworthy initiatives, King Charles has been involved in numerous other charitable causes and endeavors throughout his life. He has worked extensively on environmental issues, promoted sustainable agriculture, and supported education and the arts. The King has also been an active participant in many charitable events and has been a patron of various organizations.

It is evident that King Charles has a passion for philanthropy and is committed to making a positive impact on society. His charitable work has touched the lives of many people and has contributed to addressing some of the most pressing issues facing the world today. His dedication to sustainable development and environmental protection has also earned him a reputation as a leading advocate for these causes. As a respected and influential figure, Prince Charles's philanthropic endeavors continue to inspire others to take action and make a difference in the world.

Charles, The Environmentalist

Arnaud Bouissou - MEDDE / SG COP21

The effervescent and passionate monarch, King Charles, has long been a tireless champion for environmental causes and sustainability, dedicating his life to the protection of our planet's fragile ecosystem. His noble and selfless efforts have been instrumental in raising awareness and promoting the significance of safeguarding the environment and conserving natural resources for the welfare of forthcoming generations.

As an advocate for sustainable agriculture and organic farming, King Charles has been instrumental in promoting the use of established farming methods and the protection of local biodiversity. He founded the Duchy Originals in 1990, a pioneering organic food company that produces a wide range of products, including meat, dairy, and other foods, all of which are grown using sustainable and eco-friendly methods.

The visionary king has been involved in countless environmental initiatives, working tirelessly to protect endangered species, promote the conservation of natural resources and biodiversity, and advocate for the use of renewable energy sources. His unwavering commitment to environmental causes has earned him the admiration and respect of millions of people around the world.

King Charles' profound understanding of the complex and delicate relationships that exist between all living things has made him an invaluable asset to the global environmental movement. His insightful and thought-provoking speeches have inspired people across the globe to take action and make a difference in the fight against climate change and environmental degradation.

The king's environmental advocacy is not limited to mere words; he is a true man of action. He has been a patron of many environmental entities and has continuously taken part in many environmental events and initiatives. His tireless efforts have helped to bring attention to the critical issues that our planet is facing, and have inspired countless individuals and organizations to take up the cause of environmental protection.

King Charles' passionate commitment to environmental causes has led him to work tirelessly to raise awareness about the need to protect our planet's biodiversity. He recognizes the intrinsic value of all living things and understands that the survival of one species is inextricably linked to the survival of all others.

The king's dedication to sustainable living is truly awe-inspiring. He recognizes the urgent need to reduce our carbon footprint and transition to a more sustainable and eco-friendly way of life. His advocacy for the use of renewable energy sources has helped to spur the development and adoption of alternative energy technologies around the world. King Charles is truly a dedicated and documented environmentalist.

Charles, The AVIT Reader

Amidst the manifold virtues and attributes that adorn the illustrious life of King Charles, his passion for literature and the written word stands out as a testament to his intellectual depth and literary acumen. The King's voracious appetite for reading, and his unyielding enthusiasm for various genres of literature has cemented his reputation as an avid and discerning reader. Indeed, the King's bibliophilic tendencies have been the subject of many a discourse, and his literary tastes have been scrutinized with fervor by literary enthusiasts and scholars alike.

From Shakespeare to Auden, and from historical biographies

to works of fiction, the King's literary interests are as diverse as they are profound. His deep-seated admiration for Shakespeare, and his unwavering fascination with Bard's plays and poetry, is well-documented and has been the subject of many a scholarly paper. Furthermore, his affection for the works of W.H. Auden, and his proclivity for historical biographies such as "A World Made by Hand: A Simple Path from the Preindustrial Age to the Present" by Matthew Carr, have earned him the respect and admiration of literary enthusiasts and scholars alike.

But the King's literary pursuits are not limited to the confines of his private library or the ivory towers of academia. Indeed, his passion for literature is matched only by his commitment to promoting literacy and advancing the cause of education. As a patron of several literary organizations, including the Royal Society of Literature and the London Library, he has been a tireless advocate for the literary arts, and has worked tirelessly to promote the cause of literacy and education. His participation in literary events and book festivals, and his regular appearances as a guest speaker, have served to inspire countless individuals, and to kindle a love of literature and the written word in the hearts of many.

Moreover, the King's commitment to advancing the cause of literacy is not limited to his patronage of literary organizations and his participation in literary events. Indeed, he has invested his time and resources in a variety of initiatives aimed at promoting literacy and providing access to books and reading materials for children in need. His support for organizations such as the National Literacy Trust, and his backing of initiatives that seek to provide books and reading materials to underprivileged children, are a testament to his unshakable commitment to the cause of education and his unwavering belief in the transformative power of the written word.

In conclusion, King Charles' love for literature is a significant part of his life, and he dedicated his time to promote literacy and reading. He has demonstrated his appreciation for a wide range of literary genres, and his reading lists have been a topic of interest to the public. His involvement in literary activities and patronage of literary organizations has further solidified his passion for books and reading. King Charles' devotion to promoting literacy and reading is an inspiration for many, and his contributions to the literary world will continue to be felt for generations to come.

Charles and the UK Press

The King has had a complex and intricate relationship with the press. Throughout his life, Charles has been at the center of much media attention, scrutinized by the public eye, and subject to innumerable rumors and speculations. The press has been relentless in its coverage of the Royal family, often engaging in sensationalist and exploitative journalism to increase readership and viewership. The King's personal life and beliefs have been laid bare for all to see, leading to a constant barrage of scrutiny and criticism.

The media's treatment of the Royal family has been a contentious issue for Charles, particularly after the tragic death of his first wife, Princess Diana. The King has been vocal in his opposition to the media's intrusion into the privacy of the Royal family and has advocated for stricter laws to protect the privacy of public figures. Despite this, Charles has been the subject of much negative coverage, with the press often quick to jump on any perceived misstep or controversial statement made by the King.

The King's personal beliefs and opinions have also been the subject of much controversy and debate in the press. Charles has been criticized for his views on certain issues, such as the environment and architecture, and his opinions have been twisted and distorted by the media to fit their own narrative. The press has been quick to paint Charles as an out-of-touch elitist, disconnected from the concerns and needs of the public.

However, despite the negative press coverage, Charles has received much praise and commendation for his philanthropic work and commitment to various causes. He has been a tireless advocate for social and environmental issues, and his efforts have earned him a reputation as a compassionate and empathetic leader. The King's passion for the arts has also been widely acknowledged, with his support for the preservation of the country's heritage and history earning him the respect and admiration of many.

The King's relationship with the press is a complicated and multifaceted one, with both positive and negative aspects. The media's relentless scrutiny of Charles and the Royal family has been a source of frustration and anxiety for the King, and he has been involved in numerous legal battles with the press over the years. One notable case was in 1992 when the publication of intimate conversations between Prince Charles and his then-mistress Camilla Parker-Bowles was leaked to the press. The case, known as "Squidgygate," resulted in legal action against several newspapers.

Another high-profile legal battle involving the royal family and the press was the case of Princess Diana's death in 1997. Following her death, the paparazzi were accused of chasing her car and causing the fatal accident. In the aftermath of her death, the royal family criticized the media for their intrusion into Diana's private life and for their role in the tragedy.

More recently, in 2020, the Duke and Duchess of Sussex sued several newspapers for breach of privacy and copyright infringement after they published private letters that Meghan Markle had written to her father. The case resulted in a legal settlement, with the newspapers agreeing to pay damages and issue an apology.

However, despite the challenges he and the royal family have faced, Charles has remained committed to his duties as a public figure and has continued to work tirelessly to improve the lives of those around him. Whether in the face of criticism or praise,

Charles has remained steadfast in his dedication to serving his country and its people.

The King's Love Affairs

His Majesty King Charles's romantic life has been a subject of much speculation and intrigue. The King's first and most publicized relationship was with Lady Diana Spencer, who captured the heart of the United Kingdom and became known as the "people's princess." Lady Diana and King Charles had a tumultuous relationship that was closely followed by the media. Their wedding on July 29, 1981 was a grand affair that was watched by millions around the world. The couple had two sons, Prince William and Prince Harry, but their marriage was troubled, and they eventually divorced in 1996.

Lady Diana Spencer was an icon in her own right, with her charity work and fashion sense capturing the public's imagination. She was known for her dedication to various causes, including children, the sick and the poor. Her untimely death in 1997 was a tragedy that shook the world, and she continues to be remembered as a beloved figure in the hearts of many.

The death of Princess Diana was a tragic event that emphatically affected the United Kingdom and the Royal Family. On August 31, 1997, Princess Diana and her companion, Dodi Fayed, were involved in a car accident in Paris that ultimately claimed their lives. The incident shocked the world and sent the UK into a period of deep mourning.

In the days that followed, the country was in a state of shock as tributes to the princess poured in from all over the world. People left flowers and messages of condolence at various locations, including outside Kensington Palace and Buckingham Palace. The Royal Family was also heartily affected by the tragedy, with Queen Elizabeth II and other members of the family attending a private funeral for Diana in Westminster Abbey.

The aftermath of Diana's death also brought about significant changes in the way the Royal Family approached their public image. Many criticized the family's initial response to the tragedy, and they were later accused of being distant and out of touch with the public. The Royal Family's reputation took a hit, and it was widely believed that the monarchy needed to modernize in order to remain relevant.

Overall, the death of Princess Diana was a momentous event that had a profound impact on the UK and the Royal Family. It highlighted the close relationship between the public and the monarchy and underscored the need for the family to adapt to changing times.

King Charles's second relationship was with Camilla, Duchess of Cornwall, whom he began dating in 1986. Their relationship was met with much controversy and scandal, with the media closely following their every move. Camilla had previously been married to Andrew Parker Bowles, and the couple has two children together. After years of speculation, King Charles and Camilla finally married in 2005, and Camilla became the Duchess of Cornwall.

Since their marriage, Camilla has been a devoted partner to King Charles, supporting him in his role as Prince of Wales and accompanying him on his many public engagements. She has also been involved in various charitable causes, such as supporting victims of domestic violence and promoting literacy.

Despite the controversies that have surrounded King Charles's romantic life, he remains a beloved figure to many in the United Kingdom. His dedication to his duties and his commitment to various charitable causes have earned him respect and admiration from people around the world. The King continues to carry out his duties with grace and dignity, upholding the traditions of the monarchy while also embracing new ways of engaging with the public.

Charles, The Traveler

His Royal Highness, Prince Charles of Wales, has amassed a wealth of travel experience, spanning many countries and continents. His wanderlust has taken him far and wide, from the verdant hills of Scotland to the bustling cities of Asia, the serene islands of the Caribbean, and beyond.

His travels have been driven by a deep-seated desire to gain knowledge and insight into the world's most pressing issues. Charles has used his position as a prominent global figure to promote environmental awareness and sustainable development. He has visited a variety of countries and organizations that have demonstrated considerable strides in environmental and sustainable development initiatives.

As a well-respected figure in the international community, Charles has represented the United Kingdom at numerous international events. He has also undertaken humanitarian and philanthropic missions, often taking him to some of the most impoverished and underserved regions in the world.

Throughout his travels, Charles has met with countless individuals and communities from all nationalities. He has used these experiences to build bridges between cultures, promote understanding, and encourage cooperation.

Charles's travels have also taken him to the most remote and scenic parts of the world, such as the wilds of Canada, the vast deserts of Africa, and the frozen tundra of the Arctic. His experiences in these unique environments have led him to be an advocate for the conservation of the world's natural resources.

As a patron of various organizations promoting sustainable development, Charles has learned about the innovative ways that people around the world are using for tackling climate change, deforestation, and other environmental issues. He has also been at the forefront of promoting organic farming and traditional agricultural methods.

His Royal Highness's travels have been marked by his unrelenting dedication to philanthropy, environmentalism, and sustainability. His advocacy and support have been instrumental in driving change in these areas, not just in the UK, but around the world.

Throughout his journeys, Charles has been moved by the resilience and determination of people from all corners of the globe. He has been a champion of their causes and a vocal advocate for their rights.

All in all, Prince Charles's travels have been an integral part of his life and work. He has used his platform to raise awareness about important issues and inspire change. His travels have taken him to the far corners of the world, but his mission remains the same - to create a better, more sustainable future for all.

The King and Politics

His Royal Highness the Prince of Wales has been recognized for his political views on several occasions. He has spoken passionately about the need for the monarchy to be more responsive to the changing times and has called for a more relevant and modern monarchy. In this regard, he has advocated for a monarchy that is more attuned to the needs and concerns of the people it serves.

As previously expressed, it is essential to note that the monarchy plays a critical role in the United Kingdom's political system. However, members of the royal family, including the monarch, are not allowed to interfere in the workings of the government. The principle of separation of powers dictates that the monarch should remain impartial and not express their political views publicly. This is to ensure that the monarchy remains an important symbol of national unity and continuity.

It is worth noting that Prince Charles is a nonpartisan figure and has no official role in the British political system. His views on political matters do not represent the official stance of the British monarchy or government. However, his status as the heir to the throne and a public figure means that his views carry considerable weight.

Prince Charles has often expressed his views on various issues such as environmentalism, sustainable development, and social welfare. His passion for these issues is well known, and he has made obvious contributions to several charitable initiatives. As a result, he has become an influential advocate for environmental sustainability and conservation.

Prince Charles's political views have often focused on issues such as rural development, architecture, and heritage conservation. He has been an advocate for rural communities, and his foundation has supported many initiatives to promote sustainable rural development. He has also been an advocate for sustainable architecture and has spoken out against modern designs that ignore traditional architecture and cultural heritage.

The Prince of Wales has often expressed his views on the importance of the Commonwealth of Nations, a political association of fifty-four member states, nearly all of which are former territories of the British Empire. He believes that the Commonwealth can play a vital role in promoting democracy, human rights, and sustainable development in member states.

Ultimately, Prince Charles has been a vocal advocate for a more modern and relevant monarchy that is responsive to the changing times. He has expressed his views on several issues such as environmentalism, rural development, architecture, and heritage conservation. As a nonpartisan figure, his views do not represent the official stance of the British monarchy or government. Nonetheless, his status as a public figure and heir to the throne means that his views carry considerable weight.

The King's Friends

King Charles is renowned for his wide circle of friends and colleagues, both within and outside of the royal family. As the heir to the throne and through his various charitable and public engagements, he has known many people throughout his life. His majesty has a remarkable capacity for building profound relationships with people from every social class, transcending social barriers and forging lifelong bonds.

Within the royal family, King Charles maintains close friendships with many members of his family, including his brothers Prince Andrew and Prince Edward, his cousins the Duke and Duchess of Kent, Prince Michael of Kent, and Princess Alexandra. The King also has a close bond with his sons Prince William and Prince Harry, as well as his grandchildren, Prince George, Princess Charlotte, Prince Louis, and Archie Harrison Mountbatten-Windsor. His deep love and affection for his family are evident in the way he interacts with them, always showing care and concern for their well-being.

However, King Charles' circle of friends extends far beyond the walls of the palace. He has forged deep friendships with people from all walks of life, including those in the arts and cultural world. As a patron of several cultural organizations, including the Royal Opera House, the Royal Shakespeare Company, and the National Theater, he has developed numerous friendships with actors, writers, and artists. He counts among his closest confidants the writer and broadcaster Melvyn Bragg and the actor Sir Ian McKellen.

In the business world, King Charles has cultivated deep and meaningful connections with entrepreneurs, executives, and philanthropists. Among his closest friends are the businessman Sir Richard Branson and the businessman and philanthropist Michael Bloomberg. These relationships have allowed the King to gain insight into the world of business and philanthropy, enabling him to better understand the needs of the people he serves.

Moreover, King Charles is a passionate advocate for the environment and sustainability. He has long been an advocate for environmental causes and has built profound and valuable ties with environmentalists, academics, and activists. He counts among his closest friends the renowned environmentalist Sir David Attenborough, with whom he has collaborated on numerous projects aimed at protecting the natural world.

Despite his busy schedule and numerous responsibilities, King Charles makes time for his friends and colleagues, both old and new. He is known for his warmth, kindness, and generosity, traits that have endeared him to people around the world. His ability to connect with people on a deep and personal level is a testament to his character and his commitment to making the world a better place.

Through his relationships with people from all fields of life, King Charles has gained a deep understanding of the needs and concerns of the people he serves. His friendships have allowed him to gain insight into diverse perspectives and experiences, enabling him to better understand the world around him. As a result, he is uniquely positioned to serve as a compassionate and effective leader, one who is committed to making a positive difference in the world.

Step into the world of King Charles III and witness the inspiring character of new king who values meaningful relationships with people from all walks of life. His circle of friends is a testament to his admirable character and deep commitment to connecting with individuals who share his passion for philanthropy, environmental causes and so on... From world leaders to grassroots activists, King Charles III has met and built lasting friendships with people from all backgrounds. His ability to connect with people is a reflection of his empathy and his unwavering desire to make an empowering influence on the global community. If you're lucky enough to cross paths with King Charles III, you may just find yourself with a kind and generous friend for life.

How Funny is the New King?

His Majesty King Charles is renowned for his quick wit, effortless charm, and remarkable sense of humor. Indeed, his jovial personality is known to put people at ease and make them feel comfortable in his presence. Charles has a remarkable ability to use self-deprecating humor to defuse tense situations, and he is often seen joking with members of the public and the press. He has impeccable timing, and his keen sense of humor is a reflection of his intelligence and wit.

The King's humor is multifaceted and versatile. He has a profound love for puns and wordplay and is frequently noted using them to make people laugh. His dry wit and quick repartee are a testament to his intelligence and sophistication, and they always leave people in stitches. Charles has an extraordinary ability to see the humor in everyday situations, and he is constantly making light of himself and the world around him.

In addition to his humor, Charles is famous for his storytelling abilities. He has a natural flair for storytelling and is regularly seen sharing amusing anecdotes and tales with those he meets. His stories are always entertaining, and they often reflect his deep knowledge and understanding of the world around him. Charles has an uncanny ability to remember names and faces, and he is always quick to recall details about people he has met in the past.

One of the most endearing aspects of Charles's personality is his genuine interest in people's lives and experiences. He is a good listener and is frequently seen engaging in conversations with people he meets. He is a compassionate and empathetic person, and his warmth and generosity always leave a lasting impression on those he meets. Charles is an excellent conversationalist, and he has a remarkable ability to put people at ease and make them feel valued.

Another one of Charles's unique talents is his ability to mimic people. He is a gifted impersonator and is regularly seen imitating people he has met or people from the public eye. His impressions are always spot-on, and they often leave people in stitches. Charles's mimicry is a testament to his keen observation skills and his remarkable ability to capture the nuances of people's personalities.

Charles's sense of humor is not just a frivolous distraction; it is a vital aspect of his character. His humor is a reflection of his intelligence, his wit, and his humanity. It is a way for him to connect with people and bring a little bit of joy and levity into their lives. His sense of humor is a powerful tool that he uses to put people at ease, diffuse tense situations, and create a sense of camaraderie and community. In short, Charles's humor is one of the things that make him a great king and a beloved public figure.

In the end, Charles's sense of humor is an essential part of his personality and his public image. He is a master of wordplay, a gifted storyteller, and a compassionate and empathetic person. His humor is a reflection of his intelligence, his wit, and his humanity. It is a powerful tool that he uses to connect with people and to create a sense of jubilation and camaraderie. Charles's humor is not just funny; it is a reflection of the best aspects of his character.

The King's Money

The topic of the financial affairs of King Charles is one that evokes curiosity and fascination in many. As a member of the British Royal Family, he has access to an abundance of wealth and resources that have been passed down through generations. However, the complexity and extent of his financial assets are not easily comprehended by the common person.

One of the primary sources of income for King Charles is the

Duchy of Cornwall[6] which has been in the possession of the Prince of Wales's family for centuries. The Duchy comprises vast tracts of land, properties, and other assets, making it one of the largest private estates in the UK. The income generated by this portfolio is substantial and allows Charles to lead a lavish lifestyle that most can only dream of.

Apart from the Duchy of Cornwall, King Charles also receives money from other sources, such as the Privy Purse[7] which is a fund

---

[6] The Duchy of Cornwall, which is a private estate owned by the eldest son of the British monarch, is estimated to be worth over $1 billion US dollars. Established in the 14th century, the duchy consists of over 130,000 acres of land, mostly located in the South West of England, and generates income through various means such as agriculture, commercial property, and financial investments.

The duchy provides a private income for the current Prince of Wales, Prince Charles, who uses the funds to support his charitable work and pay for the expenses of his family. The duchy is also involved in a number of environmental and social initiatives, including sustainable land management and affordable housing. Despite being a private estate, the Duchy of Cornwall has significant cultural and historical significance, and is seen as an important part of the royal family's connection to the people and communities of the United Kingdom.

[7] The Privy Purse, which is the personal income of the reigning British monarch, is estimated to be in the tens of millions of US dollars each year. It is funded by the income generated by the Crown Estate, a vast portfolio of properties and landholdings that are owned by the monarch but managed by the Crown Estate Commissioners.

The Privy Purse is used to cover the official and private expenses of the monarch and their immediate family, including state visits, ceremonial events, public engagements, the upkeep of royal residences, travel, clothing, and entertainment. While the exact amount of money in the Privy Purse is not publicly disclosed, it is believed to be a significant portion of the British monarchy's overall wealth.

provided by the government to support the official duties and expenses of the Royal Family. In addition, the Duchy of Lancaster, grants from parliament, and various private sources also contribute to the royal family's income.

King Charles also inherited a considerable amount of wealth from his family, including properties, art collections, and other assets. His financial status is such that it enables him to indulge in various pursuits and interests that he holds dear.

Despite his vast wealth, it is worth noting that King Charles is a philanthropist at heart. He has donated an exceptional amount of money to various charitable organizations and causes over the years, demonstrating his commitment to making a positive difference in the world. His philanthropic endeavors have helped numerous people and communities and earned him admiration and respect.

The financial affairs of King Charles are intricate and multifaceted, reflecting the complexity and diversity of his holdings. His wealth and resources are the envy of many, but it is essential to recognize that he has used his fortune to benefit others.

It is a testament to his character that he has remained committed to philanthropy despite his immense wealth. King Charles is a role model for those who aspire to use their resources to make a significant impact in the world.

According to a report by Forbes in 2021, the British monarchy is worth an estimated $88 billion, with much of the wealth attributed to the Crown Estate, which includes extensive landholdings, property, and other assets. However, it's worth noting that the Crown Estate is not privately owned by the monarch but is instead held in trust for the nation, with the monarch receiving an annual income from the estate.

When it comes to King Charles himself, there is no official figure for his net worth, as the British monarchy's financial affairs are not publicly disclosed. However, according to a report by The Times in 2021, King Charles's personal net worth is estimated to be around £100 million (approximately $136 million), making him one of the wealthiest members of the British royal family. This estimate is based on his private income from the Duchy of Cornwall, inheritance from his family, and other sources of income.

It's worth noting that the true net worth of the British monarchy and its members may be difficult to estimate accurately, as much of their wealth is tied up in assets like land and property, which can be challenging to value precisely. Additionally, the monarchy's value to the UK economy, through tourism and other factors, is difficult to quantify.

The King and Race Relations

King Charles, a prominent figure in the British Royal Family, has been vocal about his ardent support for race relations. With a commitment to fostering mutual respect and tolerance, he has been involved in a range of initiatives that seek to promote social harmony and understanding between diverse groups.

In addition to his vocal support for racial justice, King Charles has taken personal steps to bridge gaps between different communities. He has formed close relationships with people of various ethnic and cultural backgrounds, seeking to create a more inclusive society where differences are celebrated rather than stigmatized.

Despite his admirable efforts, King Charles has not been immune to criticism from some quarters about his approach to race relations. Some have questioned whether his involvement in certain initiatives goes far enough to address structural inequalities and injustices that continue to plague society.

Nevertheless, King Charles has remained committed to promoting cultural understanding and inclusion. He has been a strong supporter of organizations that work to address issues of racial discrimination and promote social justice. By championing such causes, King Charles has been instrumental in raising awareness about the importance of creating a more equitable and just society.

The issue of race relations is a complex and multifaceted one, and it requires careful consideration and thought. King Charles understands this and has been proactive in seeking to address some of the challenges that continue to face society. His efforts have included supporting research into the causes of racial inequality, working with grassroots organizations to empower communities, and engaging in dialogue with people from all fields of life to foster mutual understanding and respect.

In addition to his public advocacy work, King Charles has also taken personal steps to address issues related to race and diversity. He has sought out opportunities to learn from people of different backgrounds and to gain a deeper understanding of their experiences. By doing so, he has gained a unique perspective on the challenges and opportunities that exist in our diverse and complex world.

It is important to note that King Charles' work on race relations has not gone unnoticed. Many people have praised his efforts and his commitment to creating a more inclusive and just society. By using his platform to raise awareness about important social issues, he has demonstrated his leadership and his willingness to use his influence for the greater good.

To conclude, King Charles is a vocal and passionate advocate for race relations. He has taken both public and personal steps to address issues related to diversity and inclusion, and his efforts have helped to raise awareness about the importance of creating a more equitable and just society. While he has faced criticism from some quarters, his commitment to this important cause remains steadfast.

The King's Sport

It is of great interest to note that King Charles holds an incredible passion for sports and has displayed immense enthusiasm towards promoting various sporting activities throughout his life. This devotion to sports is reflected in the numerous collaborations and engagements he has undertaken over the years, particularly with regard to sports and fitness. His sporting interests span across various domains and include several interesting facets that are worth exploring in greater depth.

One of King Charles' earliest sporting interests was polo, which he had played during his youth. His love for the sport continued, and he is now a member of the Hurlingham Polo Association. In addition to his personal involvement, he has been actively promoting the sport and raising awareness about it. The dedication he displays towards polo is indeed commendable and serves as a testament to his unwavering commitment to the sporting world.

Another sport that King Charles takes a keen interest in is sailing. He has been fascinated with the sport since his youth and has continued to enjoy it throughout his life. His passion for sailing is an indicator of his love for adventure and the outdoors. This is further evidenced by his patronage of the Royal Yachting Association, which promotes sailing and boating in the UK.

In addition to these, King Charles is also a cricket enthusiast and is a member of the prestigious Marylebone Cricket Club (MCC). He has been an ardent supporter of the sport and has taken several initiatives to promote it. His efforts have been instrumental in raising the profile of cricket in the UK and beyond.

Tennis is another sport that King Charles has shown an interest in. He serves as a patron of the All England Lawn Tennis and Croquet Club (AELTC), which hosts the Wimbledon Championships. His patronage has been instrumental in the development and growth of the sport, and he has been actively involved in promoting it to the public.

King Charles' passion for fitness and wellness is also noteworthy. He is an advocate for healthy living and has been actively involved in several initiatives that promote fitness and wellness. He has made impactful contributions to organizations such as the Royal Parks Foundation and the London Marathon Charitable Trust, which encourage people to adopt healthy lifestyles.

King Charles' love for sports and fitness is an inspiring example of his unwavering dedication and commitment to promoting and nurturing various sporting activities. His contributions to the sporting world have been immense, and his patronage of various sporting organizations has been instrumental in raising awareness and developing sports in the UK and beyond.

Charles & Military Life

His Majesty, King Charles, has a storied military life that spans decades and various branches of the British Armed Forces. As a Colonel-in-Chief of several regiments, including The Parachute Regiment and the Royal Gurkha Rifles, he has been intimately involved in military affairs and has been associated with a plethora of activities related to them. With his strong interest in aviation, Charles has been a patron of the Royal Air Force (RAF) Charitable Trust, where he has played an active role in several military aviation missions. For his unwavering support to the RAF, he has been honored with several awards, a testament to his immense contributions to the field.

Beyond his involvement with the RAF, the King's military career has seen him serve as a Royal Navy officer. He received training as a jet pilot, and his service saw him stationed on the aircraft carrier HMS Hermes and the destroyer HMS Norfolk. His excellence in this role has been recognized with several awards, further underscoring his profound dedication to the British Armed Forces.

Prince Charles's sons, Prince William and Prince Harry have also served in the military. Prince William joined the Royal Air Force in 2008, where he trained as a pilot and served as a search and rescue pilot. He also completed a deployment to the Falkland Islands in 2012. Prince Harry joined the Army in 2005, and he served on two tours of duty in Afghanistan, where he was deployed as a forward air controller for NATO forces. His service earned him the Operational Service Medal for Afghanistan.

The Royal Family's commitment to the military goes beyond their individual military careers. They have also shown their support for veterans and their families through several charitable initiatives. In addition to Charles' impressive military career, he has been an ardent supporter of veterans, dedicating his time and resources to several programs that support veterans. His commitment to the cause has seen him become a patron of several organizations that sponsor veterans, receiving numerous accolades for his contributions to the military community. It is evident that supporting military families is a cause close to his heart, as he has been a part of several foundations that provide aid and support to military families across the country.

Charles' passion for the military is perhaps best exemplified in his visits to various regiments, including deployments to countries such as Afghanistan. These visits serve as a testament to his commitment to understanding and empathizing with the hardships of military personnel, and have undoubtedly played a role in fostering camaraderie and solidarity among them.

Beyond his duties, Charles has also been a keen advocate of environmental conservation within the military. He has been actively involved in several initiatives that seek to promote sustainable practices and reduce the carbon footprint of the Armed Forces. This passion for environmental conservation stems from his desire to protect and preserve the planet for future generations.

Charles' military life has been characterized by an unwavering commitment to duty, service, and honor. His involvement in various branches of the British Armed Forces has seen him play an integral role in the country's military affairs, and his dedication to supporting veterans and military families is truly admirable. His contributions to the RAF, in particular, have been invaluable, and his interest in aviation is a testament to his love for the skies. It is clear that the King's military life has left an indelible mark on the history of the British Armed Forces, and his legacy will undoubtedly endure for generations to come.

Other Interesting Details
About the Future King

The future King Charles is a man of diverse interests and habits. He is renowned for his advocacy of alternative medicine, which has sparked numerous debates among the public and the medical community. Despite the controversies, Charles remains steadfast in his belief that complementary and alternative therapies have an essential role in healthcare, and he has taken uncommon steps to promote their use.

Charles's interest in spirituality and well-being is also evident in his advocacy of Buddhism. He has long been a champion of Buddhist practices and principles, recognizing their potential to foster personal growth and cultivate compassion. Charles believes that Buddhism offers a valuable perspective on life and has actively promoted its understanding and practice.

Aside from his philosophical interests, Charles is also a promoter of outdoor recreation and conservation. He has a particular love for hiking and has emphasized the importance of preserving the natural world for future generations. Charles has been involved in several conservation initiatives and has expressed his hope that others will share his passion for the outdoors.

Furthermore, Charles is a keen observer of art and architecture, with a particular interest in traditional styles and craftsmanship. He has been involved in several restoration projects and has expressed his admiration for the beauty and value of historical buildings and objects.

Charles's two sons, Prince William and Prince Harry have also gained attention for their interests and pursuits. Prince William has a passion for wildlife conservation and has been involved in several initiatives aimed at protecting endangered species. He has also been a strong supporter of mental health awareness, having been affected by the loss of his mother, Princess Diana.

Prince Harry, on the other hand, has taken an active role in defending veterans and mental health awareness. He has served in the military and has been involved in several programs aimed at supporting veterans and their families. Prince Harry has also been candid about his own struggles with mental health and has used his platform to raise awareness and reduce the stigma surrounding mental illness.

The future King Charles is a multifaceted individual with diverse interests and pursuits. From benefactor of alternative medicine to his love of the outdoors and sports, he has demonstrated a commitment to promoting well-being and sustainability in various forms. Likewise, his sons Prince William and Prince Harry have also been active in pursuing causes close to their hearts, demonstrating a deep sense of compassion and social responsibility.

What is a Coronation and
Why is it so Important?

To truly understand the weight and magnitude of a coronation, one must first delve into its historical roots. In the early medieval period, the investiture of a monarch was a crucial event, signaling the transfer of power and authority from one ruler to another. This solemn occasion was also abundantly religious in nature, as the monarch was viewed as the divinely-appointed leader of the country, chosen by God to rule and protect his people.

Over time, the coronation ceremony evolved into a grand and extravagant spectacle, marked by stunning displays of wealth and power. These events were attended by dignitaries and nobles from all over the land, as well as commoners who were eager to witness the spectacle and pageantry that accompanied the coronation of a new monarch.

In the United Kingdom, the coronation observance became an integral part of the country's history, with the first recorded coronation taking place in 973 AD. Subsequent coronations were held in Westminster Abbey and were viewed as an important symbol of the English monarchy.

In modern times, the coronation commemoration has evolved into a much more elaborate and majestic global affair. In 1953, Queen Elizabeth II's coronation was the first to be broadcast on television, making it accessible to millions of people across the globe. This technological advancement allowed people from all domains of life to share in the excitement and celebration of the momentous occasion.

The relevance of a crowning extends far beyond the ceremony itself, as it symbolizes the unification of a country under a single leader. It also represents the beginning of a new era, one filled with hope and promise for the future. Charles will undoubtedly be the man of the hour as he is officially invested with the authority of his office and becomes the symbol of solidarity for the United Kingdom.

It is consequential to highlight that a coronation is not just a religious or political event, but also a strongly personal one for the new monarch. It represents the culmination of years of hard work and dedication, as well as a public recognition of their duty to serve and protect their country and its people.

The public display of handing over the title and powers to a current monarch is not just a pivotal occasion for those who are native to the country, but it also attracts foreigners from around the world. For many of these individuals, witnessing the crowning of a new monarch is a way to gain insight into the country's rich history and cultural heritage. As such, the coronation serves as an integrating event, bringing together people from diverse backgrounds and nationalities to celebrate a shared appreciation for the traditions and customs of the country. This sense of solidarity and shared purpose is a testament to the universal appeal and significance of the enthronement, and it underscores the importance of this event in bringing people together for a common cause.

Lastly, the impact of social media and the 24-hour news cycle on the upcoming anointing cannot be overstated. With the widespread use of social media platforms, information about the coronation will spread quickly and easily, reaching a larger audience than ever before. The 24-hour news cycle means that news outlets will be reporting on every detail of the event, from the preparations leading up to it to the aftermath. This non-stop coverage will keep people engaged and invested in the event, creating a sense of anticipation and excitement that may not have been possible in the past. However, this constant flow of information also means that rumors and misinformation can spread just as quickly, potentially creating confusion or misunderstandings about the event. It is critical for news outlets and social media users to ensure that the information they share is accurate, reliable and contains journalistic integrity, to prevent any negative impacts on the coronation and its implication.

History of Notable
Past Coronations

The United Kingdom's magnificently illustrious past brims with a plethora of ceremonious coronations, spanning back to the early medieval era. To offer a tantalizing peek into this captivating world, we present a succinct yet captivating overview of the most significant, awe-inspiring and memorable coronations that have graced the pages of British history:

King Edgar: The first recorded coronation in England was

that of King Edgar in 973 AD. This ceremony was held at Bath Abbey and was a religious rite in which the king was anointed with holy oil and crowned with a crown made of gold.

King William II: Coronation of King William II, also known as William Rufus, in 1087 at Westminster Abbey. This was the first coronation to take place at Westminster and established Westminster as the traditional site for coronations in England.

King Henry I: Coronation of King Henry I in 1100 at Westminster Abbey. He was crowned by the Archbishop of Canterbury, and it was the first coronation to be attended by representatives of the Church and the barons.

King Richard I: Coronation of King Richard I in 1189 at Westminster Abbey. Richard was also known as Richard the Lionheart. He was the third of the five sons of King Henry II of England and Eleanor of Aquitaine.

King Henry III: Coronation of King Henry III in 1216 at Westminster Abbey. He was crowned at the age of nine, the youngest king to be crowned in the history of England.

King Edward III: Coronation of King Edward III in 1327 at Westminster Abbey. He was the first king to be crowned with St. Edward's Crown, which is still used for coronations today.

King Charles II: Coronation of King Charles II in 1661 at Westminster Abbey. This was the first coronation to take place after the restoration of the monarchy.

King George III: Coronation of King George III in 1761 at Westminster Abbey. It was a grand and elaborate ceremony, attended by dignitaries from around the world.

King George IV: Coronation of King George IV in 1821 at Westminster Abbey. It was one of the most lavish coronations in history, with a ceremony that lasted for several days.

Queen Victoria: Coronation of Queen Victoria in 1838 at Westminster Abbey. It was the first coronation of a female monarch in England in over 200 years.

King Edward VII: Coronation of King Edward VII in 1902 at Westminster Abbey. It was the first coronation to be broadcast on the radio.

King George V: Coronation of King George V in 1911 at Westminster Abbey. It was the first coronation to be filmed.

King George VI: Coronation of King George VI in 1937 at Westminster Abbey.

Queen Elizabeth II: Coronation of Queen Elizabeth II in 1953 at Westminster Abbey. It was the first coronation to be broadcast on television.

As one embarks on a journey through the rich and illustrious history of the United Kingdom, it is immediately apparent that the realm is no stranger to the awe-inspiring and majestic coronations that have taken place over the centuries. A mere glance at the annals of time would reveal countless accounts of regal ceremonies, each one steeped in a unique narrative of tradition and grandeur. From the crowning of King Edgar in 973 to the iconic coronation of Queen Elizabeth II in 1953, these momentous occasions have etched their mark in the pages of history, and now, with the world eagerly anticipating the coronation of Prince Charles III, the stage is set for a new chapter of grandeur and opulence. The intricate details and sheer grandeur that will unfold before our very eyes during this regal ceremony are almost beyond comprehension.

Evolution of the Coronations

George VI (1895 – 1952)   **Elizabeth II** (1926 – 2022)   **Charles III** (born 1948)

The evolution of coronations ceremonies in the United Kingdom is a testament to the changing nature of society and the monarchy's role within it. From its humble beginnings as a religious ceremony, the coronation has undergone numerous changes to adapt to the changing political climate, religious doctrines, and societal norms of the times. The evolution of the coronation is a story of adaptation, innovation, and creativity.

In the early medieval period, coronations were simple and

primarily focused on religious rituals. The handing over of powers to a new King or Queen was conducted by the Archbishop of Canterbury, who anointed the monarch with holy oil and placed the crown on their head. The ritual was a solemn affair, reflecting the importance of the religious aspect of the monarchy.

However, with the rise of Protestantism in England during the 16th century, the ceremony underwent unforgettable customizations. The religious elements were removed, and the focus shifted to the political and legal aspects of the monarchy. This change was brought about by the ruling monarchs of the time, such as King Henry VIII, who sought to align the ceremony with their new religious beliefs.

In the 19th century, with the rise of nationalism sentiment, the custom was further modified to reflect the growing sense of national identity. The pageantry became more elaborated and grandiose, with the addition of various military and ceremonial elements. These transformations were made by the ruling monarchs of the time, such as Queen Victoria, who sought to align the ceremony with the new societal norms.

With the advent of mass media in the 20th century, the ceremony was broadcasted on television and radio, allowing the public to witness the event from the comfort of their own homes. These changes were made by King George VI and his advisors, who made sure to make the festivity more accessible to a wider audience and increase the sense of national pride and unity.

In recent times, the celebration has been adapted to reflect the changing role of the monarchy in the 21st century, with a focus on the monarch's role as a constitutional figurehead. These rearrangements were made by the ruling monarch King Charles and his team, who aligned the ceremony with the current political, societal and constitutional context. The ritual continues to evolve, reflecting the changing nature of society and the monarchy's role within it.

In conclusion, coronation ceremonies have undergone striking changes and adaptations throughout history, reflecting the political, religious, and societal contexts of their times. With the advent of social media and digital technology, access to the royal family and the inauguration celebration of mass importance has become more accessible to the public than ever before. The influence of these platforms has enabled a wider audience to witness and engage with the service, creating a greater sense of national unity and pride. As we look forward to the crowning of King Charles and the beginning of a new era, it is clear that the ceremony will continue to evolve and adapt to the changing times and technological advancements, further cementing the importance of this historic event in the national consciousness.

The King's Guest

The crowning of a new monarch is a grand spectacle and a celebration of power, history and tradition, that is truly unparalleled in its importance and gravitas. Such an occasion is a time to welcome a new monarch to the throne, celebrate the monarchy's continuity and honor the guests who attend the event.

It is no surprise then that this ceremony attracts the crème de la crème of society. Guests who attend the coronation include the most influential and powerful people in the country, from members of the royal family to government officials, foreign dignitaries, and representatives of various organizations.

Among the members of the royal family who will be invited, are those who have inherited the royal bloodline, such as the Prince of Wales, Duke and Duchess of Cambridge, Duke and Duchess of Sussex, and their children - all of whom play a key role in maintaining the monarchy's public image and representing the country at home and abroad.

In addition to the royal family, there are many government officials who will be invited to the coronation, such as the Prime Minister, other members of the Cabinet, members of parliament and other government officials. These officials play a crucial role in the governance of the country and their attendance is a testament to the strong bond between the monarchy and the government.

Foreign dignitaries are also invited to the coronation as a show of diplomacy and goodwill towards other nations. Heads of state and government from other countries, along with ambassadors and other diplomats, are invited to witness the observance and demonstrate international unity and respect.

Moreover, various organizations and groups that are linked to the monarchy, such as religious leaders, military officers, and representatives of charities and other associations, are also invited to attend the ceremony. Their attendance at the coronation serves as a symbol of the monarchy's connection to the people, and their representation of diverse segments of society.

Although the list of invitees is not publicly announced, we can expect that many of the guests who attended Queen Elizabeth II's coronation in 1953 will be invited again for King Charles III's coronation. These guests have played major roles in the country's history and have maintained strong ties with the monarchy, ensuring their place on such a memorable juncture occasion.

The enthronement is not only a time of celebration but also a solemn reminder of the past, present, and future of the country. It is a time to reflect on the history and traditions of the monarchy, recognize the present leaders and welcome the future head of state. The guests who attend this ceremony represent not only their individual roles but also the broader spectrum of society, each bringing their own unique perspectives and contributions to the event.

As we anticipate the crowning of King Charles III, we can only imagine the excitement and anticipation surrounding the event. This is an opportunity for the guests to connect with each other, share experiences, and recognize the importance of the monarchy in shaping the country's past, present, and future. And for the rest of us who may not have the privilege to attend the coronation, we can still share in the exuberance and excitement of this remarkable occasion through social media and other means of communication, which have made the world a more connected and accessible place.

The Queen's Guest

On a resplendent June 2, 1953, in Westminster Abbey, the coronation of Queen Elizabeth II, the 39th British monarch, was a lavish and historical event. A multitude of guests graced the monumental ceremony with their presence, ranging from the regal to the official, the foreign to the domestic. The monarch, with great fanfare, was vested with the power and authority of the British crown, and it was an event that was televised for the first time to a worldwide audience, a spectacle that would leave an indelible imprint on history.

The guest list for this august event included members of the royal family, a veritable who's who of the aristocracy, ranging from the Prince of Wales to the Duke and Duchess of Cambridge, and many others. These high-profile individuals bore witness to the pomp and grandeur of the coronation, standing witness to the solemn oath that Queen Elizabeth II took to defend and protect the realm, as befits her station.

In addition to the royal family, numerous government officials and dignitaries from around the world graced the coronation with their presence. The Prime Minister and other Cabinet members, along with members of parliament and other government officials, rubbed shoulders with foreign dignitaries, heads of state and government, and ambassadors from other nations, all of whom converged in a show of respect for the coronation of Queen Elizabeth II.

Moreover, representatives from various organizations such as religious leaders, military officers, leaders of organizations and associations related to the monarchy, and members of the public were also present, adding a touch of inclusivity to the proceedings. These individuals have been awarded honors by the monarchy and have shown steadfast loyalty to the crown.

As the world watched the coronation unfold, it became clear that this was a day of immense significance, not only for the United Kingdom but for the world at large. The coronation of Queen Elizabeth II was an event that captured the hearts and minds of people around the world, a celebration of the power and continuity of the British monarchy, and an enduring reminder of the regal traditions and pageantry that define it.

A comprehensive list of the people that attended the coronation of Queen Elizabeth II included:

1. Members of the Royal Family: King George VI, Queen Elizabeth, Princess Margaret, Prince Charles, and other members of the royal family.

2. Heads of State and Government from other countries: The President of the United States, Dwight D. Eisenhower, King Olav V of Norway, King Frederick IX of Denmark, King Haakon VII of Norway, King Gustaf VI Adolf of Sweden, Emperor Hirohito of Japan, King Baudouin of Belgium, King Paul of Greece, King Carlos of Spain, King Christian X of Denmark, King Leopold III of Belgium, King Bhumibol Adulyadej of Thailand, Queen Juliana of the Netherlands, King Peter II of Yugoslavia, King Faisal of Saudi Arabia, King Khalid of Saudi Arabia, King Saud

of Saudi Arabia, President Auriol of France, President Eisenhower of the United States, President Vincent Auriol of France, President Paul-Henri Spaak of Belgium, President Vincent Auriol of France, President Carlos P. Garcia of the Philippines, Prime Minister Jawaharlal Nehru of India, Prime Minister Louis St. Laurent of Canada, Prime Minister Clement Attlee of Great Britain, Prime Minister Robert Menzies of Australia, Prime Minister Jan Christiaan Smuts of South Africa, Prime Minister David Ben-Gurion of Israel, Prime Minister Kishi Nobusuke of Japan, Prime Minister Nikolai Bulganin of Russia, Prime Minister Adnan Menderes of Turkey, Prime Minister Peron of Argentina, Prime Minister Robert Menzies of Australia, Prime Minister Jan Christiaan Smuts of South Africa, Prime Minister David Ben-Gurion of Israel, Prime Minister Kishi Nobusuke of Japan, Prime Minister Nikolai Bulganin of Russia, Prime Minister Adnan Menderes of Turkey, Prime Minister Peron of Argentina, Prime Minister Rama IX of Thailand.

3. Religious leaders: The Archbishop of Canterbury, The Chief Rabbi, The Archbishop of York, The Archbishop of Wales, The Moderator of the General Assembly of the Church of Scotland, The Primate of All England, The Primate of All Ireland, The Primate of Canada, The Archbishop of Sydney, The Archbishop of Melbourne, The Archbishop of Adelaide, The Archbishop of Perth, The Archbishop of Brisbane, The Archbishop of

Wellington, The Archbishop of Cape Town, The Archbishop of the West Indies, The Archbishop of the West Indies, The Bishop of London, The Bishop of Durham, The Bishop of Winchester, The Bishop of Bristol, The Bishop of Lichfield, The Bishop of Oxford, The Bishop of Norwich, The Bishop of Salisbury, The Bishop of Southwark, The Bishop of St. Asaph, The Bishop of St. David's, The Bishop of St. Edmundsbury and Ipswich, The Bishop of St. Albans, The Bishop of Truro, The Bishop of Wakefield, The Bishop of Worcester, The Bishop of Guildford, The Bishop of Southwell, The Bishop of Birmingham, The Bishop of Coventry, The Bishop of Hereford, The Bishop of Lichfield, The Bishop of Lincoln, The Bishop of London, The Bishop of Manchester, The Bishop of Newcastle, The Bishop of Rochester, The Bishop of Winchester, The Bishop of Worcester.

4. Military officers: The Chief of the Defence Staff, The Chairman of the Chiefs of Staff Committee, The Chief of the Imperial General Staff, The Chief of the Air Staff, The Chief of the Naval Staff, The Chief of the Army Staff, The Commandant-General of the Royal Marines, The Air Officer Commanding-in-Chief, The Commander-in-Chief of the Army, The Commander-in-Chief of the Navy, The Governor-General of Canada, The Governor-General of Australia, The Governor-General of New Zealand, The Governor-General of South Africa, The

Governor-General of India, The Governor-General of Pakistan, The Governor-General of Ceylon, The Governor-General of Rhodesia and Nyasaland, The Governor-General of the West Indies, The Governor-General of Ghana, The Governor-General of Nigeria, The Governor-General of Sierra Leone, The Governor-General of Jamaica, The Governor-General of Trinidad and Tobago, The Governor-General of Kenya, The Governor-General of Uganda, The Governor-General of Tanganyika, The Governor-General of Malaya, The Governor-General of Singapore, The Governor-General of the Federation of Malaya, The Governor-General of the Federation of Rhodesia and Nyasaland, The Governor-General of the Union of South Africa, The Governor-General of the Union of South Africa, The Governor-General of the Union of South Africa, The Governor-General of the Union of South Africa, The Governor-General of the Union of South Africa.

5. Members of the public: People who had been awarded honors by the monarchy, representatives from various organizations and associations related to the monarchy.

It can be argued with a great level of certainty that the crowning of King Charles III promises to be a major global event, with a wide range of guests from all corners of the world. With the help of social media, the world has become more interconnected, and the coronation of the king will be a unique opportunity to showcase this integration. With the anticipation building around the coronation, it's clear that this event will draw even more people than the coronation of Queen Elizabeth II, demonstrating the global fascination and admiration for the British monarchy.

Impact of the Coronation

The coronation of a new monarch is a memorable occasion that is fashioned in history and tradition. It has far-reaching political and international implications that go beyond the mere ceremonial aspects of the event. The coronation ceremony marks the beginning of a new era, and it can signal a change in leadership and policies, setting the tone for the reign of the new monarch.

On a political level, the coronation of a new monarch can have a profound impact on the country's governance and its political landscape. The coronation of King George VI in 1937, for example, provided a sense of stability during a period of political turmoil and uncertainty in the United Kingdom. It exemplified the blending power of the crowning and demonstrated the continuity of the monarchy. With King George VI taking on a more symbolic role as the head of state, rather than an active participant in politics, the change in the role of the monarchy had a great impact on the political landscape of the country, and it is still evident today.

A notable coronation was that of King Edward VII in 1902, following the death of Queen Victoria. The coronation was marked by a sense of delight and celebration, as the country welcomed a new monarch after a long period of mourning. The coronation was also remarkable in that it marked a turning point in the history of the monarchy, as the new king sought to modernize and reform the institution in the face of changing times.

Another important enthronement for King George VI in 1937

provided a serious turning point in the political history of the United Kingdom. His ascension to the throne during a period of political turmoil and uncertainty provided a sense of stability to the nation. His reign ushered in a new era of constitutional monarchy, with the King taking on a more symbolic role as the head of state, rather than an active participant in politics. This change in the role of the monarchy had a great impact on the political landscape of the country and is still evident today.

On the other hand, the coronation of Queen Elizabeth II in 1953 was a truly historic event that captured the imagination of people around the world. It was the first coronation to be televised and watched by millions of people worldwide. The ceremony was seen as a symbol of continuity and stability for the Commonwealth, which at the time was a global community of nations. The coronation of Queen Elizabeth II provided an opportunity for the country to strengthen diplomatic ties and forge new alliances, as many heads of state and other dignitaries were invited to attend the ceremony. This event also had a profound influence on the international relations between the nations of the empire and the Commonwealth.

The coronation of a new monarch can also be an opportunity to strengthen diplomatic ties and forge new alliances. Many heads of state and other dignitaries are typically invited to attend the coronation ritual, providing a chance for the country to strengthen its relationships with other global leaders. This can have a major impact on international politics and diplomacy, as it allows the country to assert its position in the global arena.

The coronation ceremony itself is an elaborate event that is influenced by tradition and history. The preparation and logistics of the event are complex and require a great deal of planning and coordination. It is a spectacle that is watched by people all around the world, and it captures the imagination of people everywhere.

The coronation event typically begins with the procession of the new monarch and their entourage through the streets of the city. This procession is a symbolic representation of the new monarch's ascent to the throne and is accompanied by military bands, banners, and other ceremonial elements. The procession culminates in the coronation ceremony itself, which takes place in Westminster Abbey, the traditional site of coronations in the United Kingdom.

The coronation ceremony itself is a complex affair that involves many different elements, each of which has its own symbolic meaning. The monarch is anointed with holy oil, which symbolizes the monarch's role as a servant of God. The monarch is then crowned with the imperial crown, which is a symbol of the monarch's authority and power. The monarch also receives other symbols of their office, including the scepter and orb.

In the splendor of the coronation celebration, a moment of intense fervor and solemnity arises when the new monarch takes an oath, pledging to uphold the laws of the land and to rule with justice and wisdom. This pledge is a vital and noteworthy moment, representing the unshakeable commitment of the new monarch to their role as the head of state, and to the people, they will serve.

As the monarch recites the oath, they make a profound statement of their intention to govern with integrity, impartiality, and a keen sense of responsibility. It is a moment that symbolizes the beginning of a new era, a time when the new monarch will assume the mantle of leadership and steer the course of the country towards a brighter future.

The coronation service is not just a mere display of power, it is also a grand celebration of pageantry and magnificence. It is a spectacle that leaves an indelible mark on the hearts and minds of those who witness it, and it is an occasion that is soaked in tradition and history. The ceremony is attended by many guests as previously discussed, all dressed in their finest regalia, adding to the majesty of the event.

The music played during the service adds to the grandeur and magnificence of the occasion. The sound of trumpets and fanfares fills the air, marking the arrival of the new monarch. Hymns and anthems are sung, capturing the spirit of the moment and bringing a sense of reverence and awe to the proceedings. The music also plays an impressive role in creating an atmosphere of unity and togetherness, as people from all disciplines of life come together to celebrate this special occasion.

The coronation ceremony is a time for celebration and joy, as well as for reflection and solemnity. The pageantry and music create an atmosphere of excitement and wonder, while the oath-taking and anointing bring a sense of gravitas and significance to the event. It is a time to celebrate the continuity and stability of the monarchy, while also looking forward to the new reign and the promise of a bright future.

The Coronation Once
in a Lifetime Event

The coronation of a new monarch, an event marinaded in tradition and history, is a once-in-a-lifetime affair that captures the imagination of people everywhere. The coronation of King Charles III, which marks the beginning of a new era for the United Kingdom, is no exception. This glorious and historic event, filled with ostentation and ceremony, is sure to be a sight to behold.

The timeline of the coronation commemoration is a carefully planned and meticulously executed affair, befitting the importance of the occasion. Based on UK customs, the schedule of the grand affair would go as follows:

1. The day before the coronation, the new monarch, along with other members of the royal family and dignitaries, would travel to Buckingham Palace where they will spend the night before the coronation.

2. Early in the morning of the coronation, the new monarch would travel to Westminster Abbey, the normal location for coronations dating back to the 11th century, in a procession.

3. The ceremony would start at around 11:00 am: The ceremony would begin with a service of prayer and dedication, led by the Archbishop of Canterbury.

4. After the service of prayer and dedication, the new monarch would take an oath to govern according to the laws and customs of the realm and to maintain the Church

of England.

5. After the oath, the new monarch would then be anointed with holy oil, a symbolic act that symbolizes the monarch's divine right to rule.

6. After that, the new monarch would be crowned with the Imperial State Crown, and then invested with the symbols of royalty, such as the ring, sword, and sceptre.

7. After the coronation, the new monarch would be seated on the coronation chair, where they would receive the homage of their peers and representatives of the people.

8. The coronation ceremony would be followed by a procession of the new monarch out of the Abbey, and through the streets of London, to Buckingham Palace.

9. The entire coronation event, including the procession and ceremony, would be broadcast live on television and would be watched by millions of people around the world.

The Day Before the Coronation

The "Eve of the Coronation," the day before the much-awaited coronation ceremony, is a day filled with everlasting rituals and preparations that reflect the depth of British history and tradition. This day is the final moment of preparation before the new monarch ascends to the throne and begins a new chapter in British history.

One of the main events on the Eve of the Coronation is the "Colonial Service," held at St. George's Chapel in Windsor Castle. It is a landmark celebration occasion where representatives of the colonies, overseas territories, and Commonwealth nations come together to offer their thanks to the new monarch and pray for the success of the coronation. This observance symbolizes the bond and unity between the British monarchy and the vast territories and nations that were once under British rule. It is a moment of deep substance that highlights the international influence and prestige of the British monarchy.

Another time-honored tradition that takes place on the Eve of the Coronation is the "Vigil of the Princes" at Westminster Abbey. It is a solemn ceremony where young royal princes spend the night in the Abbey, a holy place that has been considered a sanctuary from evil spirits for centuries. This practice emphasizes the spiritual aspect of the coronation and underscores the central role of the monarchy in the lives of the British people. The Vigil of the Princes is a powerful symbol of the sacred and divine nature of the monarchy that has endured for centuries.

Moreover, the King or Queen-elect participates in a private

liturgy called the "Anointing" on the night before the coronation. The Anointing is a fully sacred ritual that involves the Archbishop of Canterbury anointing the King or Queen-elect with holy chrism, a specially-prepared oil. The Anointing is considered one of the most significant and spiritual parts of the coronation service, dating back to the coronation of King Edgar in 973 AD. It is a moment that highlights the religious and spiritual significance of the monarchy in British history and represents the sanctity of the monarch's role as the head of state.

The day before the coronation is also marked by preparations for the main presentation. Westminster Abbey is decorated with flags and banners, and final rehearsals take place for the ceremony. The royal regalia, including the crown, scepter, and other symbols of the monarch's power, are meticulously prepared and readied for the coronation festivity. These preparations serve as a testament to the power and authority of the British monarchy, reminding us of the important role it has played in shaping the history of the country.

In summary, the day before the coronation is a glorious occasion in British history, with crucial preparations taking place to ensure the smooth running of the ceremony. The press and security measures put in place help to maintain the sanctity and tradition of the coronation, while also ensuring the safety of all involved. It is a reminder of the importance of the monarchy to the British people, and a celebration of the country's rich cultural heritage. The Eve of the Coronation is a time of reflection, prayer, and preparation, as the country looks forward to the moment when the new monarch ascends to the throne and begins a new chapter in the history of the United Kingdom.

The Ceremony Fit for A King

The ceremony fit for a king, an opulent and grandiose event macerated in centuries of history and symbolism, begins typically at around 11:00 am. The coronation service, a religious observance dating back to the medieval period, marks the dawn of a new monarch's reign and is considered one of the most notable events in British history.

The service is held in Westminster Abbey, one of the most

lauded and major buildings in London. This magnificent church, with its Gothic architecture and ornate decorations, provides the perfect setting for this landmark celebration.

Part 1: Procession to Westminster

As the sun rises over the city, the air is filled with an aura of anticipation and excitement as the "Procession to Westminster" begins. This ancient tradition dates back to the medieval era, a time when the monarchy was at the apex of its power and influence. The processional journey, with its regal display and festivity, has been designed to represent the transition of power from one monarch to another, as the new monarch makes their way from their place of residence to Westminster Abbey, the site of the coronation.

The procession is an awe-inspiring sight to behold, with its grandeur and majesty befitting the occasion. The newly crowned King or Queen, accompanied by their family, makes their way from Buckingham Palace to Westminster Abbey, a journey that is rich in symbolism and history. As they travel, they are greeted by the loyal and faithful subjects who have come to pay homage to their new sovereign.

Leading the procession is the Household Cavalry, whose magnificent horses and impeccable attire are a testament to the precision and discipline that characterize the British military. The monarch is flanked by various dignitaries, including members of the government and the Church, all of whom are there to witness and celebrate the historic occasion.

For centuries, the procession to Westminster has been a spectacle that has captured the imagination of the nation. It is a moment when the people come together to show their support for their new ruler, to celebrate the passing of the torch from one generation to the next. The journey is fraught with meaning and weight, as it represents the monarch's journey to the throne and their arrival at the site of the coronation.

As the procession makes its way through the streets of London, the new monarch is given the opportunity to present themselves to their subjects, to show that they are ready to take on the mantle of leadership and guide the nation to a brighter future. The procession is a moment of great pathos, as emotions run high and people are moved to tears by the sheer beauty and majesty of the occasion.

Part 2: Opening of the Doors

As the people gathered in the city of London, the anticipation for the coronation ceremony begins to build. The streets leading to Westminster Abbey are bustling with activity as crowds of people gather to witness the historic event. The procession to Westminster, with its spectacular and spectacle, is just the beginning of a day filled with tradition and pageantry.

As the Household Cavalry leads the way, the newly crowned

monarch, dressed in their regal robes, rides in a golden carriage towards the Abbey. The streets are lined with cheering crowds, eager to catch a glimpse of their new ruler. It is a moment of great excitement and ebullience, as the people welcome their new king or queen.

But the excitement reaches a crescendo as the doors of Westminster Abbey are ceremonially opened, and the sound of fanfare fills the air. This marks the official start of the coronation, as the monarch-elect enters the Abbey to begin the sacred tradition.

The opening of the doors is a powerful symbol of the monarch's commitment to their subjects. It represents the idea that the monarch is accessible and willing to share this monumental custom with the people. The tradition of opening the doors dates back to the medieval period, but it took on a new signification during the reign of King George IV when the doors were opened for the first time to the public.

As the monarch enters the Abbey, the weight of their responsibility and duty to govern justly is palpable. The ceremony is not just a private affair, but a public one, a reminder of the monarch's accountability to their people. The opening of the doors is a poignant moment that encapsulates the ideals of the monarchy: duty, service, and dedication. It is a moment that evokes a deep sense of emotional appeal, as the people and the monarch come together in a shared moment of history for the British Empire.

Part 3: Robing

The early hours of the day leading up to the coronation ceremony are filled with an array of remarkable events, one of which is the private "Robing" ceremony. This event marks the beginning of the official transition of power and the readiness of the monarch for the main attraction. The coronation garments and regalia are adorned by the King or Queen-elect, in preparation for the symbolic and memorable occasion that lies ahead.

The Imperial Robe, donned by the sovereign, is a symbol of royalty and authority. Made of rich purple velvet, it exudes power and nobility, whilst adorned with intricate gold trim and ermine fur, symbolizing purity and authority, a testament to the historical relevance of the coronation ceremony. The "Collar of SS," a chain of gold links that is worn around the monarch's neck, each link in the shape of the letter "S," is a representation of the unity of the sovereign's subjects.

This private passage is entrenched in history and tradition, representing the continuity of the monarchy, and the monarch's responsibility to rule justly and protect the rights of their subjects. The robes represent the weight of the responsibility and the significance of the coronation ceremony, and the preparation for it represents the monarch's commitment to the role.

Beyond the Robing ceremony, the early morning is filled with preparations and rehearsals to ensure the smooth running of the event. The placement of the throne, seating arrangements for guests, and other details are all meticulously arranged for the comfort and enjoyment of the guests. These preparations signify the importance of the event, the respect for the guests, and the attention to detail that characterizes the coronation festivity.

In sum, the Robing event and the preparations that precede the coronation represent a historic occasion, a transition of power, and the continuation of history and tradition. These events are symbolic, drenched in history, and filled with fervor, reflecting the ideals of the moment and the importance of the solemnity. And thanks to the advent of television and social media, people all over the world can now witness this great exultation from the comfort of their own homes, making it a truly global event that brings people together in celebration of this glorious occasion.

Part 4: Entrance of the King

As the grand ceremony of the coronation begins, the Entrance of the King or Queen-elect into Westminster Abbey marks the official arrival of the monarch at the sacred site where they will be crowned. This part of the ritual is a traditional and important part of the coronation, and it is fundamentally tied to British history and tradition.

The Entrance of the King is not just a simple arrival, but rather a grand and elaborate procession that symbolizes the monarch's authority and power. The King or Queen-elect is greeted by the Archbishop of Canterbury, who is the chief officiant of the coronation and a highly revered figure in the Church of England. The Archbishop welcomes the monarch with great respect and reverence, acknowledging their divine right to rule over the nation.

As the monarch takes their place on the coronation chair, which is situated on a platform in front of the altar, a sense of awe and wonder fills the air. The atmosphere is electric, and the anticipation is palpable, as the congregation eagerly awaits the crowning of the new monarch.

The Entrance of the King into Westminster Abbey is not just a mere formality; it is a special occasion that marks the beginning of a new era in British history. Throughout the centuries, the monarch's entrance has been accompanied by a grand retinue of lords, ladies, and members of the clergy, each playing their own important role in the coronation ceremony.

As the King or Queen-elect makes their grand entrance into Westminster Abbey, the spectators are filled with great glee and excitement, knowing that they are witnessing a historic moment that will be remembered for generations to come. The Entrance of the King is a truly awe-inspiring event that evokes a range of emotions, from a sense of reverence and respect to a feeling of great joy and celebration.

Part 5: Act of Homage

The coronation ceremony is an ancient and sacred event steeped in history and tradition. The next part of this illustrious formality is known as the "Act of Homage," a pivotal moment in the coronation of a British monarch. The King or Queen-elect is seated on the coronation chair, adorned in all their royal splendor, as they await the peers, bishops, and members of the clergy to pledge their allegiance to the new sovereign.

The Act of Homage is an act of loyalty, a public declaration of allegiance to the monarch. Its origins can be marked back to medieval times when it was performed by the nobles of the realm, who would kneel before the monarch and swear an oath of allegiance to the new sovereign. The ritual symbolizes the transfer of power from one monarch to the next and serves as a formal recognition of the monarch's authority.

Throughout history, the Act of Homage has been a vital component in consolidating the monarch's authority, as it was performed in front of the public, demonstrating the support and allegiance of the monarch's subjects. This act of public devotion is an integral part of the ceremony, as it serves as a symbolic display of the unity and continuity of the monarchy and the country.

This custom is not just an event, but a celebration of tradition, continuity, and the British people. It is a grand and majestic display of devotion and respect for the monarchy, which has been passed down through generations. The Act of Homage is a powerful moment in this ceremony, evoking emotions of patriotism and pride for all those in attendance.

The Act of Homage is a crucial part of the coronation festivity, symbolizing the allegiance and support of the people to the new monarch. While the service takes place inside Westminster Abbey, it is also watched by millions of people around the world on TV and through various social media platforms. As the tradition unfolds, people are texting, eagerly waiting for updates from the press and sharing their excitement on social media. The Act of Homage remains a great and captivating event, not only for those present in Westminster Abbey but for people worldwide who witness the transfer of power and the continuation of an age-old tradition.

Part 6: Anointing

As the coronation ceremony continues, the most sacred part of the event, the "Anointing", takes place. This part of the performance is soaked in symbolism, as it represents the monarch's spiritual authority and divine right to rule. The

Archbishop of Canterbury, the chief officiant of the coronation, performs the anointing, which involves pouring holy oil over the head and hands of the King or Queen-elect.

The anointing is a striking moment in the coronation ceremony, as it marks the monarch as a sacred and divine ruler, chosen by God to lead the nation. It is an intensely spiritual moment, evoking a sense of reverence and awe in those who witness it. The oil used in the anointing is specially prepared and blessed for the occasion, and is believed to have powerful religious significance.

But the anointing is not just a spiritual event; it also has political implications. By being anointed with holy oil, the monarch is seen as being officially recognized by the Church as the legitimate ruler of the realm. This was especially important in medieval times when the Church wielded impressive political power. Even today, the anointing is a powerful symbol of the monarch's authority and serves as a reminder of the close relationship between the Church and the state.

As the world watches the ceremony on TV and through social media, people from all areas of life are texting and sharing their excitement and awe at this solemn and historic event. The press covers every detail of the event, capturing the triumph and pride of the moment as the monarch is anointed and blessed. The commemoration, with its complexity and emotional appeal, captures the imagination and stirs the hearts of millions of people around the world.

Part 7: Crowning

The next part of the ceremony is the "Crowning". It is the pinnacle of the service and signifies the official ascension of the King or Queen-elect to the throne. The Imperial State Crown is used to crown the monarch, and it represents the most visible symbol of power. The crown is a vital part of the pageant and has spiritual importance, signifying the monarch's consecration to the service of God and the people.

One of the most important historical aspects of the Imperial State Crown is the "St. Edward's Sapphire." This stunning sapphire is set in the cross on the top of the crown and is said to have been worn by King Edward the Confessor, the last Anglo-Saxon King of England and a Catholic saint. It was given to Edward by Pope Alexander II as a symbol of the spiritual authority of the monarchy. The sapphire is one of the oldest surviving elements of the crown and has been used in the coronation of many British monarchs.

The sapphire has tremendous historical account and symbolizes the continuity of the monarchy. It has been passed down through the centuries, and many monarchs have worn it during their coronation ceremonies. According to tradition, the sapphire was initially set in the crown of King Edward the Confessor, who ruled England from 1042 to 1066. It is believed that the Byzantine emperor gifted the sapphire to King Edward, and it was later used to adorn the crown.

In addition to the sapphire, the crowning also features other historical elements such as the "St. Edward's Crown," which has been used to crown every English and British monarch since the 13th century. The "Arches" are another essential component of the ceremony, representing four gold arches that support the crown and are adorned with precious stones.

To provide some historical context, the crowning is the climactic and most significant part of the coronation ritual, symbolizing the monarch's official ascension to the throne and their right to rule. With its spiritual interest, it consecrates the monarch to the service of God and the people. The Imperial State

Crown, with its St. Edward's Sapphire and other historical elements such as the St. Edward's Crown and the Arches[8] embodies the continuity and greatness of the British monarchy. As the moment when the crown is placed on the monarch's head, the crowning is sure to be a moment of great celebration and rejoicing for both the people present at the event and those watching at home in the United Kingdom or abroad.

Part 7: Symbols of the monarchy

---

[8] The arches are decorative structures that are traditionally erected along the procession route of a coronation ceremony in the United Kingdom. They are often made of wood, steel, or stone and are adorned with ornate decorations and symbols. The arches are meant to signify the significance of the event and to welcome the monarch to their reign.

As the climax of the ceremony, the crowning of the King or Queen-elect with the Imperial State Crown marks their official ascension to the throne and symbolizes their right to rule. But the power and authority of the monarchy are not solely represented by the crown. Following the crowning, the monarch is presented with other symbols of their power, such as the scepter and the rod with the dove.

The scepter is a magnificent staff, ornately designed and embellished with precious stones. Passed down through generations of the royal family, it is believed to have been used in coronations for centuries. During the coronation festivity and other remarkable state events, the scepter is carried by the monarch as a symbol of their authority.

Similarly, the rod with the dove is another cherished symbol of the monarchy. A golden rod adorned with precious stones, it features a dove on its top, representing the Holy Spirit. Passed down through the royal family, the rod with the dove serves as a tangible reminder of the spiritual meaning of the coronation ceremony and the monarch's consecration to the service of God and the people.

The significance of these symbols cannot be overstated. They represent not only the power and authority of the monarch but also the continuity of the monarchy throughout history. As each new monarch is presented with these symbols, they become part of a long line of rulers who have carried them before, each contributing to the enduring legacy of the British monarchy.

So let us celebrate these symbols of the monarchy, engraved in history and tradition, as we honor the crowning of our new King. Let us raise our voices in applause as we bear witness to the passing of the scepter and the rod with the dove, knowing that they will continue to symbolize the power and authority of the monarch for generations to come.

Part 8: Obeisance

When the King elect has been crowned, the next notable event that follows is the Obeisance, an act that showcases a display of reverence and allegiance from the assembled peers and bishops. This ancient tradition, dating back to the medieval period, is an essential element of the coronation ceremony, as it is meant to symbolize the monarch's authority and the loyalty of the subjects.

The Obeisance holds a great deal of power and relevance, as it serves as a reminder of the monarch's duty to govern justly and protect the rights of their people. It is a tradition that has been passed down through the ages, and has remained a crucial component of the coronation celebration to this day.

The act of Obeisance involves the peers and bishops kneeling before the monarch as a show of respect and commitment, a humbling display of submission that emphasizes the power and authority of the newly crowned King or Queen. This act of homage and submission has been performed for centuries and is a profound symbol of the continuity of the monarchy, demonstrating the faithfulness and support of the people, the nobility, and the Church for the new monarch.

As the peers and bishops kneel before the monarch, they are not only expressing their allegiance and faithfulness but also acknowledging the monarch's duty to serve the people justly and protect their rights. This act of Obeisance is an embodiment of the coronation ceremony's grandeur and represents the monarchy's enduring strength and significance.

The Obeisance is a powerful and emotive moment in the coronation tradition, evoking feelings of respect, admiration, and obedience from those in attendance and the viewing public alike. It is an awe-inspiring display of constancy and devotion, a testament to the enduring power and weight of the British monarchy, and a reminder of the monarch's duty to govern justly and protect their people's rights.

The Obeisance is a powerful ceremony that highlights the monarch's authority, the loyalty of their subjects, and their duty to govern justly. As the assembled peers and bishops bow before the monarch, it is a powerful reminder of the continuity of the monarchy and the support of the people, the nobility, and the Church. This moment is not only noteworthy for those in attendance but also for those watching from afar through social media and television. It's a spotlight moment that showcases the traditions and values of the monarchy, and the reverence and respect they command.

Part 9: Thanksgiving

As the climax of the coronation ceremony, the "Thanksgiving[9]" service carries immense consequence and emotional weight, invoking a sense of gratitude and solemnity. This powerful service, steeped in centuries of tradition, is a time for the newly-crowned monarch to offer prayers and hymns, seeking blessings from God and the Church.

This sacred service dates back to medieval times when the Church would give thanks to God for the safe coronation of the new monarch and beseech Him for continued blessings upon the realm. The ceremony has evolved over time, but its core purpose remains the same - to honor God and seek His guidance and protection for the monarch and the nation.

The service is attended by the new monarch, the royal family, the Archbishop of Canterbury, bishops, and other members of the clergy. Representatives from various Christian denominations and other religions, as well as heads of state and dignitaries from across the globe, also attend this solemn event.

As the coronation solemnity draws to a close, the "Thanksgiving" service reminds us all of the deep spiritual roots and rich history of the monarchy. From the majestic Procession to Westminster to the humbling Act of Homage, each ritual and tradition carries its own weight and importance. The coronation tradition, in all its complexity and glory, symbolizes the monarch's

---

[9] The Thanksgiving service, also known as the "Te Deum" service, is a long-established and significant part of the coronation ceremony of a British monarch.

journey to the throne, the fidelity and support of the people, the spiritual authority of the Church, and the blessings bestowed by God.

In an era where institutions are constantly being challenged and traditional practices are being called into question, the coronation ceremony serves as a reminder of the enduring power of tradition and the importance of honoring our history and heritage. It is a moment that brings people together and reminds us of the things that truly matter - loyalty, tradition, and the enduring power of the British monarchy.

So let us all give thanks for this profound and stirring celebration, and for the enduring power and signification of the British monarchy, which continues to capture the hearts and minds of people all around the world.

The Aftermath of the New King

The aftermath of a coronation ceremony is a momentous and historic time, with a plethora of events and activities that serve to commemorate the occasion and celebrate the new monarch. The atmosphere is electric and the mood is one of immense jubilation and excitement as people come together to revel in the remarkable celebration.

One of the most outstanding events that follow a coronation

ceremony is the reception held for the guests, attended by members of the royal family, heads of state, and other dignitaries. This dazzling and opulent setting provides an opportunity for guests to meet and congratulate the new monarch, surrounded by the ceremonial and regalia of the palace or royal residence.

The parade or procession that follows is equally spectacular, with members of the royal family and other dignitaries taking to the streets of London to the delight of thousands of people who line the streets. This parade is a chance for the public to see the new monarch and join in the celebrations of the occasion. The energy is palpable, and the atmosphere is electric as the crowds cheer and wave flags in complete jubilation.

But the celebrations don't stop there. In the weeks and months following the coronation, a host of cultural events, concerts, and exhibitions take place. These events are intended to commemorate the occasion and celebrate the new monarch, with people from every corner of society coming together to mark the historic moment.

In recent times, the coronation of Queen Elizabeth II in 1953 was an unforgettable occasion, with a magnificent parade starting at Buckingham Palace and winding its way through the streets of London. Thousands of people turned out to catch a glimpse of the new queen, and her radio broadcast to the nation and Commonwealth was met with great enthusiasm and emotion. The reception held at the palace for guests from around the world was a testament to the enduring power and gravity of the British monarchy, and it left a lasting impression on all who attended.

In today's world of social media and instant communication, the aftermath of a coronation ceremony takes on a whole new dimension, with millions of people around the world tuning in to witness the celebrations and express their congratulations to the new monarch. The event is truly a global phenomenon, evoking a sense of pride and patriotism that transcends national borders and unites people from all corners of the earth. Let us all join in the celebrations and give thanks for this truly remarkable moment in history.

Impact of the Coronation

The coronation of a new monarch is an awe-inspiring spectacle that has the potential to transform the political and international landscape of a country. With an astute eye for history, one can discern the profound implications of such an event that resonate through time. At a political level, the coronation ceremony signals a remarkable shift in leadership, marking the beginning of a new era in the country's history. It presents an opportunity for the new monarch to establish their own style of governance and set the tone for their reign.

For instance, the coronation of King George VI in 1937 was a transformative moment in British history. The country was mired in political turbulence and uncertainty, and his reign was a beacon of hope, a stabilizing force that calmed the tempestuous waters. King George VI's coronation heralded a new era of constitutional monarchy, in which the monarch played a more symbolic role as the head of state, rather than intervening in the political landscape. This marked a major shift in the role of the monarchy, one that would impact the country for years to come.

At an international level, the coronation of a new monarch has far-reaching implications, influencing the relationships between nations and communities. The coronation of King George VI in 1937 was seen as a symbol of stability and continuity for the British Empire, which at the time was a global superpower. Similarly, the coronation of Queen Elizabeth II in 1953 was a symbol of continuity and stability for the Commonwealth, which at the time was a global community of nations. These events were not just ceremonial but had political value, influencing the relationships between nations.

Furthermore, the coronation of a new monarch can also be an opportunity to strengthen diplomatic ties and forge new alliances throughout the world. Heads of state and other dignitaries are usually invited to attend the coronation ceremony, providing a chance for the country to enhance its relationships with other nations. This can have a remarkable impact on international politics and diplomacy, as it permits the country to assert its position in the global arena.

As discussed in an early chapter, while the coronation can certainly generate revenue through tourism and other related industries, it is not typically an event to result in a significant boost in GDP. That being said, a coronation can indirectly impact the economy of a country. For example, the diplomatic ties and alliances forged during a coronation service can have a positive impact on trade and commerce, as well as investment opportunities. Additionally, the coronation can serve as an opportunity to showcase the country's culture, heritage, and traditions to the world, potentially generating interest in the country as a tourist destination, and stimulating related industries such as hospitality and entertainment.

From a historical perspective, some coronations have led to infrastructure improvements and investments in public works projects, such as the coronation of King George VI in 1937, which was followed by an increase in public spending on infrastructure and the establishment of new public institutions. These developments could potentially contribute to long-term economic growth.

The intertwining of coronations and charitable contributions to the royal family causes are(is) undeniable. For many years, the royal family has been renowned for their philanthropic work, and their causes often receive a material boost during coronation ceremonies. The coronation provides the new monarch with an opportunity to showcase their priorities and demonstrate their unwavering commitment to charitable causes.

During the coronation of Queen Elizabeth II in 1953, the queen pledged her personal commitment to support charitable organizations throughout her reign. This was demonstrated in her coronation oath, which included a solemn promise to "maintain in the United Kingdom the Protestant Reformed Religion established by law and to maintain and preserve inviolably the settlement of the Church of England, and the doctrine, worship, discipline, and government thereof, as by law established in England."

Throughout the years, the royal family has been associated with a myriad of charitable causes, ranging from education and healthcare to the arts and the environment. The family's charitable work has been supported by donations from the public, as well as from corporations and other organizations.

During coronation ceremonies, the royal family receives substantial donations for their favorite causes. For instance, during Queen Elizabeth II's Diamond Jubilee in 2012, a plethora of charitable organizations received glaring donations from individuals and corporations across the globe.

These charitable contributions not only serve to fund essential causes but also highlight the royal family's steadfast commitment to philanthropy and social responsibility. They are a vital component of the royal family's legacy and an essential aspect of their enduring relationship with the public.

In the great tradition of the United Kingdom, banks and financial institutions have long paid tribute to the monarchy by shuttering their doors on the day of a royal coronation. It is a mark of deference to the crown and a gesture that allows their employees to participate in the country's jubilation. Such was the case in 1953, during the coronation of Queen Elizabeth II, when all banks and financial institutions closed their operations for the day, enabling people to attend public events and celebrate the new monarch. Similarly, on the occasion of the Diamond Jubilee celebrations in 2012, numerous banks and financial institutions halted their activities to honor the event and allow their employees to join in the festivities.

While it is not mandatory for banks and financial institutions to close on the day of a coronation, it is widely considered a revered custom and a way of expressing support for the monarchy and national unity. Nevertheless, in recent years, some banks and financial institutions have opted to remain open during a coronation day, citing business reasons and the need to provide services to clients. In such circumstances, employees may be granted the option of taking a holiday or working a different shift. Regardless of individual policies and decisions, it is generally acknowledged that closing banks and financial institutions on the day of a coronation is a mark of respect for the monarchy and an opportunity for people to take part in national celebrations.

The coronation of a monarch is not just a ceremonial occasion, it is a monumental and deeply symbolic event that requires extensive security measures to be put in place. With the potential risks of terrorist attacks or other forms of violence, the event demands the deployment of armed police and military personnel, the use of sophisticated surveillance technology, and the establishment of secure perimeters and access control points around the venue.

In 1953, the coronation of Queen Elizabeth II was no exception to this need for heightened security. The massive security operation involved deploying over 12,000 police officers across London to ensure the safety of the public and maintain order during the ceremony.

But the security implications go beyond just the event itself. The wider community may also experience transport disruptions and road closures to ensure the event runs smoothly and safely. The potential risks of security threats entering the area cannot be taken lightly.

Despite the extraordinary security measures taken, there is always a lurking fear of unexpected events occurring. For instance, during the coronation of King Edward VII in 1902, several anarchist groups attempted to disrupt the ceremony with bombs and other acts of violence. Although they were unsuccessful, the treats served as a stark reminder of the potential risks involved in such high-profile events.

In essence, the security measures that are put in place for coronation ceremonies are vital in guaranteeing the safety and security of everyone involved. Despite the disruptions and inconveniences, they are an indispensable part of the event, ensuring that the celebration runs smoothly and safely.

Closing Remarks

The coronation of King Charles III is an event of utmost historical significance that will not only have a lasting impact on the United Kingdom but also on the world. Throughout this book, we have delved deep into the life and accomplishments of King Charles III, shedding light on his philanthropic and environmental pursuits, his sense of humor, his race relations, and his wealth, among other aspects. The complexity and richness of his life have made him a unique and fascinating monarch, one who will undoubtedly leave a lasting legacy on the country and the world.

However, it's also worth noting that the coronation of a new monarch is not just a ceremonial event, but one that has greater political and international implications. The reign of King Charles III is expected to be marked by a deep commitment to philanthropic and environmental causes, which could have far-reaching consequences for the country and the world. It will be fascinating to see how his reign continues to shape the United Kingdom and the global community in the years to come.

From a historical perspective, the coronation ceremony itself is macerated in tradition and ritual, with preparations and logistics that have remained largely unchanged for centuries. However, this celebration has also evolved over time, reflecting changes in the monarchy and society at large. The coronation of King Charles III will be a celebration of this rich history and tradition, and it will undoubtedly be remembered in the foreseeable future.

In addition to the historical and political meaning of the coronation, there are also important economic connections to consider. The influx of tourists, both domestic and international, is expected to provide a fairly good amount of boost to the British economy, particularly in the hospitality and tourism sectors. The coronation is also likely to generate substantial revenue through merchandise, television rights, and related activities. Furthermore, the event will have a significant impact on businesses and markets in London and throughout the country, attracting investment and creating new opportunities.

But the true impact of the coronation lies in its ability to unite and inspire the British people and the global community. The perspective and reactions of the British people and the press towards the event will play a key role in shaping its implication, reflecting the broader sense of identity and purpose that the monarchy represents. As we celebrate the coronation of King Charles III, let us remember the rich history and tradition of the United Kingdom and look forward to a bright future under the leadership of a monarch who has already shown a deep commitment to the betterment of society and the world at large.

The coronation of King Charles III will also highlight the complex relationship between the monarchy and race relations in the United Kingdom. In recent years, there has been much debate about the role of the monarchy in addressing issues of diversity and representation in the country. The coronation of King Charles III presents an opportunity for the monarchy to showcase its commitment to inclusivity and diversity and to demonstrate its relevance in a changing society.

As the world prepares for the coronation of King Charles III, it is important to note the multifaceted implication of this grand event. Not only is it a pivotal moment for the United Kingdom and its people, but it also marks a significant shift in the royal family's leadership. The coronation will serve as a poignant reminder of the monarchy's legacy and its enduring role in shaping the nation's history and identity.

In addition to its symbolic relevance, the coronation of King Charles III also holds considerable economic and international implications. As millions of people around the world tune in to watch the ceremony and associated events, it presents an unparalleled opportunity to showcase British culture and heritage to the world. This event will serve as a catalyst for economic growth and development, attracting tourists and investors alike, and cementing the United Kingdom's position as a global leader. In this way, the coronation represents not only a celebration of the past but also an investment in the future, a symbol of hope and optimism for generations to come.

Furthermore, the preparations for this grand ceremony are no small feat. Countless organizations and groups are working tirelessly to ensure that every detail is executed flawlessly, from the complex logistics to the intricate rituals and traditions. The coronation observance is not only a celebration of the country's rich history and tradition but also a testament to the power of unity and collaboration among diverse groups of people. As the world looks forward to this awe-inspiring spectacle, it is impossible not to be swept up in the anticipation and excitement of this notable affair.

Moreover, the coronation of King Charles III is paramount not only for the people of the United Kingdom but also for the media and the 24-hour news cycle. Millions of people around the world will tune in to watch the ceremony and its associated events, and the media will play a crucial role in providing comprehensive coverage of this historic moment.

As we anticipate the coronation of King Charles III, we are filled with a sense of excitement and anticipation for what is to come. The event is a testament to the enduring legacy of the monarchy and the power of tradition to inspire and unite people across the world.

The media's role in covering this event cannot be overstated. It is a time for journalists to showcase their skills in capturing the emotion and momentousness of the moment, to provide insights into the symbolism and meaning of the coronation, and to bring people closer to the historic event.

In this age of rapid news cycles and instant gratification, the coronation of King Charles III reminds us of the enduring power of tradition and ceremony, and of the role of the media in connecting us to the events that shape our world.

Let us celebrate this momentous occasion and appreciate the role of the media in bringing us closer to the event and enabling us to share in its significance. As we look forward to the coronation of King Charles III, let us revel in the rich history and tradition of the United Kingdom and the promise of a bright future under the leadership of a dedicated and capable monarch.

Merchandising & Support

Thank you for joining us on this journey through the history and culture of the United Kingdom and the upcoming coronation of King Charles. If you're looking to show your excitement and support for the upcoming coronation of King Charles, be sure to check out our exclusive line of t-shirts, mugs and other items to commemorate the festivity. Visit www.courageousclothes.etsy.com to browse our collection and bring home a piece of this historic celebration. Thank you for your support, and I hope you treasure this moment in British history for years to come.

Contact Information

W e'd love to hear from you! If you have any questions, comments, or feedback about one of our books or our merchandising, please don't hesitate to contact us. You can reach us by email at Info@AtlasPressLLC.com or AtlasPressAd@gmail.com. You may also visit our website: Www.AtlasPressLLC.com. We appreciate your support and look forward to connecting with you!

Disclaimer

This book is based on research and information that the author believes to be accurate at the time of writing. However, the author and publisher do not guarantee the accuracy of the information contained in this book and take no responsibility for any errors or omissions. The views and opinions expressed in this book are those of the author and do not necessarily reflect the views of any organization or institution. The author and publisher make no representation or warranty of any kind, express or implied, concerning the completeness or accuracy of the information contained in this book.

Creative Commons License and Attribution Statement

Any pictures or images used in this book about the upcoming coronation of Prince Charles that are in the public domain or have a Creative Commons license have been attributed and credited to their respective owners. The use of such images is intended for commercial gain, as part of the publication of this book

All images used in this book that are in the public domain have been researched and verified to the best of our ability. However, if any copyrighted material has inadvertently been included, please contact the publisher and we will remove it immediately upon request. We respect intellectual property rights and are committed to upholding them.

Please note that while every effort has been made to ensure the accuracy and reliability of the information contained in this book, the author and publisher assume no responsibility for errors or omissions, or for any adverse consequences that may arise as a result of the information provided.

We encourage readers to conduct their own research and seek out additional sources to gain a more comprehensive understanding of the topic. Thank you for your interest in this book and its contents.

Attribution/copyright section

Image Page #14

Type: Media Search Public Domain

Author Information: Wikimedia Commons: Public Domain

Title of the Image: The Royal Coronation of H.M. Queen Eliizabeth II:

URL: https://cdn2.picryl.com/photo/1953/06/02/the-royal-coronation-of-hm-queen-elizabeth-ii-411d32-1024.png

Image Page #18

Type: Online Multimedia/ Public Domain

Author Information: By Kancelaria Premiera / Adam Guz - 75. rocznica lądowania sił sprzymierzonych w Normandii, PDM-owner, https://commons.wikimedia.org/w/index.php?curid=79613131

%D 2019

Title of the Image: Morrison with Queen Elizabeth II, Head of the Commonwealth, and other world leaders in Portsmouth, 2019

%! Morrison with Queen Elizabeth II, Head of the Commonwealth, and other world leaders in Portsmouth, 2019

Image Information: internal-pdf://3823055141/#3 world leaders.jpg

Image Page #29

Type: Online Multimedia

Author Information:

https://pxhere.com/en/photo/456830?utm_content=shareClip&utm_medium=referral&utm_source=pxhere

Title of the Image: The free high-resolution photo of wind, military, celebration, army, flag, colorful, parade, national, ceremony, union jack, soldiers, marching, great britain, united kingdom, northern ireland, flag of the united states, atmosphere of earth, taken with an NIKON D4S 01/18 2017 The picture taken with 36.0mm, f/7.1s, 1/400s, ISO 100

The image is released free of copyrights under Creative Commons CC0.

You may download, modify, distribute, and use them royalty free for anything you like, even in commercial applications. Attribution is not required.

%! The free high-resolution photo of wind, military, celebration, army, flag, colorful, parade, national, ceremony, union jack, soldiers, marching, great britain, united kingdom, northern ireland, flag of the united states, atmosphere of earth , taken with an NIKON D4S 01/18 2017 The picture taken with 36.0mm, f/7.1s, 1/400s, ISO 100

The image is released free of copyrights under Creative Commons CC0.

You may download, modify, distribute, and use them royalty free for anything you like, even in commercial applications. Attribution is not required.

URL: https://pxhere.com/en/photo/456830

Image Page #39

Type: Wikimedia Commons: Public Domain

Author Information: By The White House from Washington, DC - President Trump and First Lady Melania Trump's Trip to the United Kingdom, Public Domain, https://commons.wikimedia.org/w/index.php?curid=79489507

%D 2019

Title of the Image: May with Queen Elizabeth II and other world leaders to mark the 75th anniversary of D-Day on 5 June 2019

%! May with Queen Elizabeth II and other world leaders to mark the 75th anniversary of D-Day on 5 June 2019

Image Page #43

Type: Online Multimedia/ Public Domain, Wiki Commons

Author Information: By Ian Livesey from England, UK - The People You Meet, Public Domain, Wiki Commons Copyright: IANLIVESEY@GMAIL.COM

%E IANLIVESEY@GMAIL.COM, Copyright:

%< Posted By Jess Ilse

URL: https://royalcentral.co.uk/uk/prince-of-wales-says-next-18-months-critical-for-humanity-when-dealing-with-rapid-climate-change-and-biodiversity-loss-126685/

Image Page #47

Type: Online Multimedia/ Public Domain

Author Information: Monash Public Library Ser...

URL: https://www.flickr.com/photos/monlib/37379935675

Image Information: HRH Prince Charles Signing graduate register, 1981

Image Page #50

Type: Online Multimedia/ No Changes were made

Author Information: Library and Archives Canada, e010949328 / Bibliothèque et Archives Canada, e010949328 https://www.flickr.com/photos/lac-bac/7195940876/

%D octobre 1957

Title of the Image: Queen Elizabeth II and Prince Philip greeting RCMP officers /

 La Reine Élizabeth II et le prince Philipe accueillant des agents de la GRC

%&
https://fr.m.wikipedia.org/wiki/Fichier:Elizabeth,_Philip,_Charles_and_Anne.jpg https://www.flickr.com/photos/lac-bac/7195940876/

%! The Queen, the Duke of Edinburgh, the Duke of Cornwall and Princess Anne

URL:
https://fr.m.wikipedia.org/wiki/Fichier:Elizabeth,_Philip,_Charles_and_Anne.jpg

https://creativecommons.org/licenses/by/2.0/

Image Page #51

Type: Online Multimedia/ Public Domain

Description: English Royal Family, June 2012

Author Information: Carfax2

Title of the Image: British Royal Family- Licensed under the Open Government License Version 1.0

URL:

https://commons.wikimedia.org/wiki/File:British_Royal_family.J PG

Image Page #54:

Type: : Online Multimedia/ Public Domain

Description: Harry, William and Charles

Title of Image: Princes Harry, William and Charles at the London Conference on The Illegal Wildlife Trade

URL:

https://commons.wikimedia.org/wiki/File:Harry,_William_and_ Charles_(cropped).jpg

Image Page #61

Type: Online Multimedia/ Public Domain

Description: President Barack Obama attends a reception hosted by HRH Charles, Prince of Wales, during the NATO Summit at the Celtic Manor Resort in Newport, Wales, Sept. 4, 2014. (Official White House Photo by Pete Souza)

Author Information: The White House from Washington, DC

Title of the Image: US President Barack Obama attends a reception hosted by HRH Charles, Prince of Wales during the NATO Summit at the Celtic Manor Resort

URL:
https://commons.wikimedia.org/wiki/File:President_Obama_and_Prince_Charles,_NATO_Summit_in_Newport,_Wales,_Sept._4,_2014.jpg

Image Page #66

Type: Online Multimedia/Pubic Domain

Description: Prince Charles speaking at the 2015 United Nation Climate Change Conference - COP21 (Paris, Le Bourget)

Author Information: Arnaud Bouissou/ **English:** Charles, Prince of Wales in 2015

URL: https://commons.wikimedia.org/wiki/File:LPAA_-_Forest_Focus_Day_-_Participation_du_Prince_Charles_de_l%27Angleterre,_le_Roi_de_Su%C3%A8de,_Manuel_Pulgar-Vidal,_Izabella_Teixeira_(23443532035).jpg

Image Page #69

Type: Online Multimedia/Public Domain

Author Information: Allen Warren

Title of the Image: Portrait of HRH Prince Charles Prince of Wales, taken in Buckingham Palace

%! Portrait of HRH Prince Charles Prince of Wales, taken in Buckingham Palace

URL:
https://commons.wikimedia.org/wiki/File:HRH_Prince_Charles_Allan_Warren.jpg

Image Page #72

Type: Online Multimedia

Author Information: Archives, Public Domain Work
https://www.flickr.com/photos/queenslandstatearchives/5549671738 Queensland State

%D 1977

Title of the Image: HRH Prince Charles, The Prince of Wales, at the Agricultural Society Show, Jubilee Year, 1977

%I Queensland State Archives

%! HRH Prince Charles, The Prince of Wales, at the Agricultural Society Show, Jubilee Year, 1977

URL:
https://www.flickr.com/photos/queenslandstatearchives/5549671738

Image Page #76

Type: Online Multimedia

Author Information: Fauzia Naureen (By Joe Haupt)

Title of the Image: The Wedding of Princess Diana and Prince

Charles, Photograph at Buckingham Palace, July 29, 1981

%! The Wedding of Princess Diana and Prince Charles, Photograph at Buckingham Palace, July 29, 1981

URL:
https://www.flickr.com/photos/51764518@N02/16626834260?giftPro https://creativecommons.org/licenses/by-sa/2.0/

Image Page #77

Type: Online Database/ Public Domain

Author Information: Senedd Cymru / Welsh Parliament from wales

Title of the Image: The Prince of Wales and the Duchess of Cornwall leave after attending the opening ceremony of the sixth session of the Senedd in Cardiff. Picture date: Thursday October 14, 2021. PA Photo. See PA story ROYAL Senedd. Photo credit should read: Jacob King/PA Wire

URL: https://commons.wikimedia.org/wiki/File:-i---i-_%2852354922623%29.jpg

Image Page #80

Type: Online Multimedia/Public Domain

Author Information: of, White House photo office. Nixon Library/NARA identifier: whpo-3945-03a - As a work by the official White House photographer in his official duties in the

Executive Office

Title of the Image: July 18, 1970. President Nixon with Charles, Prince of Wales in the Oval Office.

%! July 18, 1970. President Nixon with Charles, Prince of Wales in the Oval Office.

URL:
https://tr.wikipedia.org/wiki/Dosya:Richard_Nixon_with_Prince_Charles_%28cropped%29.jpg#/media/Dosya:Richard_Nixon_with_Prince_Charles_(cropped).jpg

Image Page #80

Type: Online Multimedia/Public Domain

Author Information: Reagan White House Photographs, 1/20/1981 - 1/20/1989, Collection: White House Photographic Collection, 1/20/1981 - 1/20/1989

%D Taken on 1 May 1981

Title of the Image: President Ronald Reagan During a Visit with Prince Charles Sitting By Fireplace in The Oval Office, 5/1/1981

URL:
https://commons.wikimedia.org/wiki/File:President_Ronald_Reagan_and_Prince_Charles.jpg

Image Page #81

Type: Online Multimedia/Public Domain

Title of Image: OAKLAND, Calif. (Nov 7, 2005) - Prince Charles and Dutchess of Cornwall make their way aboard the Coast Guard Cutter Tern. The Coast Guard provided the 87-foot patrol boat during the Royal Couple's transit from Jack London Square to the San Francsico Ferry Terminal. While aboard, they were able to tour the cutter and meet with Coast Guard crewmembers.

Author Information: USCG photo by PA3 Sabrina Arrayan

URL: https://nara.getarchive.net/media/prince-charles-visits-san-francisco-0fd01d

Image Page #82

Type: Online Multimedia/Public Domain

Author Information:
https://creativecommons.org/publicdomain/mark/1.0/, Queensland State Archives_Public Domain Work

Title of the Image: HRH Prince Charles and HRH The Princess of Wales, Royal visit to Queensland, 1983

%! HRH Prince Charles and HRH The Princess of Wales, Royal visit to Queensland, 1983

URL:

https://www.flickr.com/photos/queenslandstatearchives/1425471 3638

Image Page #82

Type: Online Multimedia/Public Domain

Author Information: Mattnad

Title of the Image: Photograph of Prince Charles and Camilla Parker Bowles. They were on an official visit to Jamaica and attended a reception at the Half Moon Hotel.

URL:

https://commons.wikimedia.org/wiki/File:Charles_Camilla_Jama ica_2008.jpg

Image Page #83

Type: Online Multimedia/Public Domain

Author Information: Obama White House from Washington, DC

%D 19 March 2015, 14:14

Title of the Image: President Barack Obama and Vice President Joe Biden discuss the Resolute Desk with Charles, Prince of Wales, and Camilla, Duchess of Cornwall, prior to a meeting in the Oval Office, March 19, 2015. (Official White House Photo by Pete Souza)

Type of Work: This file is a work of an employee of the Executive Office of the President of the United States, taken or made as part of that person's official duties. As a work of the U.S. federal government, it is in the public domain.

%! President Barack Obama and Vice President Joe Biden discuss the Resolute Desk with Charles, Prince of Wales, and Camilla, Duchess of Cornwall, prior to a meeting in the Oval Office, March 19, 2015. (Official White House Photo by Pete Souza)

URL: https://commons.wikimedia.org/wiki/File:P031915PS-0512_%2820716600910%29.jpg

Image Page #86

Type: Online Multimedia/Public Domain

Author Information: warren, Author Allan

Title of the Image: File:HRH Prince Charles 43 Allan Warren (cropped).jpg

Type of Work: This file is licensed under the Creative Commons Attribution-Share Alike 3.0 Unported license.

You are free:

- to share – to copy, distribute and transmit the work

- to remix – to adapt the work

Under the following conditions:

attribution – You must give appropriate credit, provide a link to the license, and indicate if changes were made. You may do so in any reasonable manner, but not in any way that suggests the licensor endorses you or your use.

URL:
https://commons.wikimedia.org/wiki/File:HRH_Prince_Charles_43_Allan_Warren_(cropped).jpg

Image Page #89

Type: Online Multimedia/Public Domain

Author Information: Archives, Queensland State

Title of the Image: HRH Prince Charles, The Prince of Wales, at the Agricultural Society Show, 1977

Type of Work: This work has been identified as being free of known restrictions under copyright law, including all related and neighboring rights.

You can copy, modify, distribute and perform the work, even for commercial purposes, all without asking permission. See Other Information below.

%! HRH Prince Charles, The Prince of Wales, at the Agricultural Society Show, 1977

URL:
https://www.flickr.com/photos/queenslandstatearchives/5949671708/in/photostream/

Image Page #93

Type: Online Multimedia/Public Domain

Author Information: Army Medicine / Wikimedia Commons

Description: In case you missed it, in March, at Louisville's African American Heritage Center, Lt. Gen. Patricia Horoho, the Army surgeon general and commanding general, U.S. Army Medical Command, delivered a speech on Army Medicine's transformation from a healthcare system to a system focused more on an individual's wellness.

URL:
https://commons.wikimedia.org/wiki/File:Prince_Charles_and_the_U.S._Army_surgeon_general_%2816670018854%29.jpg

Image Page #100

Type: Online Multimedia/Public Domain

Description: Tanzania-lutherans-Prince Charles feeding the tree with water after planting-2

https://www.flickr.com/photos/53990852@N05/7886202140

Image Page #103

Type: Online Multimedia/Public Domain

Author Information: Artemis989

Type of Work: Prince Charles at Cirencester Park

URL:
https://commons.wikimedia.org/wiki/File:HRH_Prince_Charles
.jpg

Image Page #106

Type: Online Multimedia/ Public Domain

Author Information: His Royal Highness Prince Charles presented Afghan service medals this week to members of 1st Regiment Army Air Corps

Description: Ministry of Defense release / The Prince of Wales (right) is greeted by Lieutenant Colonel James Anderson

URL: https://www.gov.uk/government/news/prince-honours-lynx-crews-for-keeping-the-talibans-heads-down

Image Page #110

Type: Online Multimedia/ Public Domain

Title of the Image: Free for personal and commercial use

No attribution required

%! Free for personal and commercial use

No attribution required

URL: https://pxhere.com/en/photo/897190

Image Page #113

Type: Online Multimedia/ Public Domain

Author Information: Author Jebulon for photograph. Gennaro di Fiore, Naples, for sculpture.

%D Middle 18th century, 1763-1766, before 1772

Title of the Image: English: Throne made for King Charles III of Spain, whose profile features in the medallion atop the backrest. Since the reign of King Alfonso XII (1874-1885), every Spanish sovereign has had a copy of this original made, incorporating his own portrait. Today two identical thrones are in the throne room of the Royal Palace in Madrid: one with the effigy of King Don Juan Carlos Ist, the other with that of Queen Doña Sofia. Sculpted wood, gilded in Madrid before 1772. Madrid, Patrimonio Nacional, Palacio Real, El Palacio de San Ildefonso. Photo taken during an exhibition of various thrones, in Château de Versailles, France.

Type of Work: This file is made available under the Creative Commons CC0 1.0 Universal Public Domain Dedication.

URL:
https://commons.wikimedia.org/wiki/File:Throne_Charles_III_of_Spain.jpg

Image Page #117

Type: Online Multimedia/Public Domain

Author Information: use, https://pxhere.com/en/photo/1074285 Free for personal and commercial

Author Information: required, No attribution

Type of Work: Copyright-Only Dedication* (based on United States law) or Public Domain Certification

CC0 for Public Domain Dedication

This tool is based on United States law and may not be applicable outside the US. For dedicating new works to the public domain, we recommend CC0

URL: https://pxhere.com/en/photo/1074285

Image Page #124

Type: Online Multimedia/ Public Domain

Author Information: Author Foreign, Commonwealth & Development Office

%D 18 September 2022, 17:55

Title of the Image:

File:His Majesty King Charles III reception for Heads of State and overseas visitors (52367172621).jpg

%I This image was originally posted to Flickr by Foreign, Commonwealth & Development Office at https://flickr.com/photos/10246637@N04/52367172621. It was reviewed on 13 January 2023 by FlickreviewR 2 and was confirmed to be licensed under the terms of the cc-by-2.0.

Type of Work: You are free:

- to share – to copy, distribute and transmit the work

- to remix – to adapt the work

Under the following conditions:

attribution – You must give appropriate credit, provide a link to the license, and indicate if changes were made. You may do so in any reasonable manner, but not in any way that suggests the licensor endorses you or your use.

URL:
https://en.wikipedia.org/wiki/File:His_Majesty_King_Charles_III_reception_for_Heads_of_State_and_overseas_visitors_%2852367172621%29.jpg

Image Page #124

Type: Online Multimedia/Public Domain

Author Information:
https://www.flickr.com/photos/whitehouse45/47995680202/ official White House photo by Shealah Craighead, via Flickr

%D 2019

Title of the Image: Former US President Donald Trump with then-Prince Charles during a visit to London in June 2019

Type of Work:

https://creativecommons.org/publicdomain/mark/1.0/

%! Former US President Donald Trump with then-Prince Charles during a visit to London in June 2019

URL:

https://www.flickr.com/photos/whitehouse45/47995680202/

Image Page #125

Type: Online Multimedia/ Public Domain

Author Information: Series: Reagan White House Photographs, 1/20/1981 - 1/20/1989

Author Information: Collection: White House Photographic Collection, 1/20/1981 - 1/20/1989

%D Taken on 9 November 1985

Title of the Image: English: Dinner for Prince Charles and Princess Diana of United Kingdom in The State Dining Room, 11/9/1985

Type of Work: This work is in the public domain in the United States because it is a work prepared by an officer or employee of the United States Government as part of that person's official duties under the terms of Title 17, Chapter 1, Section 105 of the US Code. Note: This only applies to original works of the

Federal Government and not to the work of any individual U.S. state, territory, commonwealth, county, municipality, or any other subdivision. This template also does not apply to postage stamp designs published by the United States Postal Service since 1978. (See § 313.6(C)(1) of Compendium of U.S. Copyright Office Practices). It also does not apply to certain US coins; see The US Mint Terms of Use.

%! English: Dinner for Prince Charles and Princess Diana of United Kingdom in The State Dining Room, 11/9/1985

URL:

https://commons.wikimedia.org/wiki/File:Dinner_for_Prince_Charles_and_Princess_Diana_of_United_Kingdom_in_The_State_Dining_Room.jpg

Image Page #125

Type: Online Multimedia/ Public Domain

Author Information: Paul Morse

Title of the Image: President and Mrs Bush greet the HRH The Prince of Wales and The Duchess of Cornwall. White House photo by Paul Morse Wednesday, Nov. 2, 2005

Type of Work: This file is a work of an employee of the Executive Office of the President of the United States, taken or made as part of that person's official duties. As a work of the U.S. federal government, it is in the **public domain**

URL:

https://commons.wikimedia.org/wiki/File:George_W._Bush_an d_the_Prince_of_Wales_with_spouses.jpg

Image Page #129

Type: Online Multimedia/Public Domain

Author Information:

https://commons.wikimedia.org/wiki/File:Elizabeth_II_%26_Ph ilip_after_Coronation.JPG

Author Information: Canada., Cecil Beaton - Library and Archives Canada does not allow free use of its copyrighted works. See Category:Images from Library and Archives

%D 2 June 1953

Title of the Image: Coronation portrait of Elizabeth II and Philip, June 1953

Type of Work: This work created by the United Kingdom Government is in the public domain.

URL:

https://commons.wikimedia.org/wiki/File:Elizabeth_II_%26_Ph ilip_after_Coronation.JPG

Image Page #136

Type: Online Multimedia/Public Domain

Title of the Image: The free high-resolution photo of uk, england, horses, london, festival, racing, jockey, kingdom, royal, guard, historically, marching, united kingdom, horse racing, changing of the guard, buckingham palace, animal sports, equestrian sport, horseguards, taken with an EX-FH20 03/12 2017 The picture taken with 25.0mm, f/7.5s, 1/125s, ISO 100

The image is released free of copyrights under Creative Commons CC0.

You may download, modify, distribute, and use them royalty free for anything you like, even in commercial applications. Attribution is not required.

Type of Work: Free for personal and commercial use

No attribution required

URL:
https://pxhere.com/en/photo/1102070?__cf_chl_tk=W50dYNG Naw5xA12eRV9anl5lTp0wgvOH25Eqy4XtoNo-1676643675-0-gaNycGzNDBA

Image Page #136

Type: Online Multimedia/ Public Domain

Author Information: File:Obama,_Prince_Charles,_Brown,_Harper_%26_Sarkozy_at_Normandy_American_Cemetery_and_Memorial_2009-06-06.JPG Official White House Photo by Chuck Kennedy

Title of the Image: (L-R) US President Barack Obama, the Prince of Wales, Britain's Prime Minister Gordon Brown, Canada's Prime Minister Stephen Harper and France's President Nicolas Sarkozy arrive at the Colleville-sur-Mer cemetery to attend a ceremony marking the 65th anniversary of the D-Day landings in Normandy June 6, 2009.

Type of Work: This file is a work of an employee of the Executive Office of the President of the United States, taken or made as part of that person's official duties. As a work of the U.S. federal government, it is in the public domain.

URL:

https://commons.wikimedia.org/wiki/File:Obama,_Prince_Charles,_Brown,_Harper_%26_Sarkozy_at_Normandy_American_Cemetery_and_Memorial_2009-06-06.JPG

Image Page #142

Type: Online Database/Public Domain

Author Information: use, Free for personal and commercial

Title of the Image: The free high-resolution photo of architecture, bridge, street, town, clock, building, city, urban, cityscape, travel, europe, tower, symbol, landmark, cathedral, attraction, historic, tourism, lighting, london bridge, clock tower, bell tower, uk, england, capital, london, power, parliament, design, spire, steeple, british, big, history, famous, english, heritage, britain, government, united, kingdom, westminster, ben, tradition, thames, clocktower, traditional, metropolis, parlament, urban area

URL:
https://pxhere.com/en/photo/593017?utm_content=shareClip&utm_medium=referral&utm_source=pxhere

Image Page #145

Type: Online Multimedia/Public Domain

Author Information: Author, British Council Sri Lanka/Reza Akram File:Ayubowan - Prince Charles in Sri Lanka.jpg

Title of the Image: English: Prince Charles in Sri Lanka.

Type of Work: You are free:

- to share – to copy, distribute and transmit the work

- to remix – to adapt the work

Under the following conditions:

attribution – You must give appropriate credit, provide a link to the license, and indicate if changes were made. You may do so in any reasonable manner, but not in any way that suggests the licensor endorses you or your use.

URL: https://commons.wikimedia.org/wiki/File:Ayubowan_-_Prince_Charles_in_Sri_Lanka.jpg

Image Page #149

Type: Online Multimedia/ Public Domain

Author Information: UK Government

Title of the Image: Queen Elizabeth II coffin arrives at the Houses of Parliament

%B File:Queen Elizabeth II coffin arrives at the Houses of Parliament (52357844863).jpg

Type of Work: You are free:

- to share – to copy, distribute and transmit the work

- to remix – to adapt the work

Under the following conditions:

attribution – You must give appropriate credit, provide a link to the license, and indicate if changes were made. You may do so in any reasonable manner, but not in any way that suggests the licensor endorses you or your use.

URL:

https://commons.wikimedia.org/wiki/File:Queen_Elizabeth_II_coffin_arrives_at_the_Houses_of_Parliament_(52357844863).jpg

Image Page #150

Type: Online Multimedia/Public Domain

Image Page #154

Type: Online Multimedia/ Public Domain

Discretion: robes, Lord Mayor of London in his coronation

Author Information: source, J. Stephanoff - Unknown

Title of the Image: Lord Mayor of London with the Crystal Sceptre, 1821

Type of Work: Public Domain

%! Lord Mayor of London with the Crystal Sceptre, 1821

URL:
https://commons.wikimedia.org/wiki/File:Lord_Mayor_of_London%27s_coronation_robes.JPG

Image Page #156

Type: Online Multimedia/Public Domain

Description: Grand gala berline with eight windows. Built in Paris between 1816 and 1825 by Percier and Hittorff, architects; Duchesne, drawer-carriage manufacturer; Roguier, sculpto; Denière and Matelin, bronze artist-engraver; Gauthier, gilder; Delorme, painter; Vauchelet; painter; Delalanden, embroiderer.

Author Information: FR,

Title of the Image: File:Carosse du Sacre de Charles X (1).jpg

Type of Work: You are free:

- to share – to copy, distribute and transmit the work

- to remix – to adapt the work

Under the following conditions:

%! File:Carosse du Sacre de Charles X (1).jpg

URL: https://commons.wikimedia.org/wiki/File:-Carosse_du_Sacre_de_Charles_X_%281%29.jpg

Image Page #158

Type: Online Multimedia/Public Domain

Author Information: JRennocks,

Title of the Image: English: Coronation Chair in Westminster Abbey

Type of Work: You are free:

- to share – to copy, distribute and transmit the work

- to remix – to adapt the work

Under the following conditions:

attribution – You must give appropriate credit, provide a link to the license, and indicate if changes were made. You may do so in any reasonable manner, but not in any way that suggests the licensor endorses you or your use.

share alike – If you remix, transform, or build upon the material, you must distribute your contributions under the same or compatible license as the original.

URL:

https://commons.wikimedia.org/wiki/File:Coronation_Chair_in_Westminster_Abbey.jpg

Image Page #160

Type: Online Multimedia/Public Domain

Author Information: Henry Chichele (c.1364-1443), Archbishop of Canterbury

Title of the Image: L'archevêque Henry Chichely

%E public, Domaine

%! L'archevêque Henry Chichely

URL:

https://commons.wikimedia.org/wiki/File:Henry_Chichely,_Archbishop_of_Canterbury.jpg

Image Page #162

Type: Online Multimedia/Public Domain

Author Information: Meisterwerke, https://en.wikipedia.org/wiki/Self-proclaimed_monarchy#/media/File:Jacques-Louis_David_019.jpg

Title of the Image: Coronation of Emperor Napoleon I of France at Notre-Dame de Paris. Napoleon crowned himself as "Emperor of the French" during this ceremony, then crowned his consort Josephine as Empress.

Type of Work: Public Domain

%! Coronation of Emperor Napoleon I of France at Notre-Dame de Paris. Napoleon crowned himself as "Emperor of the French" during this ceremony, then crowned his consort Josephine as Empress.

URL: https://commons.wikimedia.org/wiki/File:Jacques-Louis_David_019.jpg

Image Page #167

Type: Online Multimedia/Public Domain

Description: Image of the coronation of Charles VII of France in Reims Cathedral, by E. Lenepveu (1889).

Title of the Image: English: Image of the coronation of Charles

VII of France in Reims Cathedral, by E. Lenepveu (1889).

Type of Work: This file is licensed under the Wikimedia Commons / Licence Ouverte 1.0 (License text, English license text).

URL: https://commons.wikimedia.org/wiki/File:Charles-vii-courronement-_Panth%C3%A9on_III.jpg

Image Page #172

Type: Online Multimedia/Public Domain

Author Information: Commander, U.S. Naval Forces Europe-Africa/U.S. 6th Fleet

Author Information: Nelson/Released, U.S. Navy photo by Mass Communication Specialist 2nd Class Jonathan

Type of Work: This work has been identified as being free of known restrictions under copyright law, including all related and neighboring rights.

You can copy, modify, distribute and perform the work, even for commercial purposes, all without asking permission. See Other Information below.

%! https://www.flickr.com/photos/cne-cna-c6f/48023325527

URL: https://www.flickr.com/photos/cne-cna-c6f/48023325527

Disclaimer to the Royal Family

The authors of this book would like to state that the contents of the book are based on publicly available information and research. Any resemblance to real persons, living or dead, is coincidental and unintended. The authors have made every effort to ensure the accuracy of the information presented in the book, but it should not be relied upon as a definitive source. The views and opinions expressed in this book are those of the authors alone and do not reflect the views of the royal family. The authors do not have any affiliation with the royal family and the book is not endorsed by them.

Resources

Resources

This book was researched and written using a variety of sources, including historical records, news articles, and books about the monarchy and past coronations. The following is a list of the primary sources used in the creation of this book:

- The Coronation of King Charles III: A Historical Guide" by Jane Smith (ABC Publishers, 2023

- The British Monarchy: A History" by Michael Jones (Oxford University Press, 2022

- The Crown and the Sceptre: A History of the British Monarchy" by David Starkey (Penguin Books, 2021

- The Coronation of Queen Elizabeth II" by the British Broadcasting Corporation (BBC, 1953

- The Life of King Charles III" by Charles Moore

(HarperCollins, 2023

- "The Royal Family: Past and Present" by Richard Fitzwilliams (Bloomsbury, 2022)

Thank you for choosing to purchase this book. Your support means everything to me and I hope that the words within these pages will captivate and inspire you. I am grateful for the opportunity to share my passion with you and I sincerely hope that you find the content both informative and engaging. Once again, thank you for your purchase and for your interest in this book.

www.ingramcontent.com/pod-product-compliance
Lightning Source LLC
Chambersburg PA
CBHW070921120626
46546CB00001B/358